NATALIA KHARLAMPIEVA

FOREMOTHER ASIA

LONDON 2016

HERTFORDSHIRE PRESS

Published in United Kingdom
Hertfordshire Press Ltd © 2016

9 Cherry Bank, Chapel Street
Hemel Hempstead, Herts.
HP2 5DE, United Kingdom

e-mail: publisher@hertfordshirepress.com
www.hertfordshirepress.com

FOREMOTHER ASIA

NATALIA KHARLAMPIEVA ©

English - Yakut (Saha)

Translated by Svetlana Yegorova-Johnstone, Jakov Kolovskij, Lidija Grigor'eva, Ariadna Borisova, Ivan Tertychnyj

Edited by David Parry

Typeset by Akirova Akylai

Illustrations by Vasilyev V.R., Votyakov Yu.I., Karamzin V.C.

Project manager Anna Lari (Suslova)

British Library Catalogue in Publication Data
A catalogue record for this book is available from the British Library
Library of Congress in Publication Data
A catalogue record for this book has been requested

ISBN: 978-1-910886-22-9

CONTENTS

The *Marziya Zakiryanova Award*
for the Best Female Work
at Open Eurasia & Central Asia
Book Forum and Literature Festival - 2015

MARZIYA NURTAZOVNA ZAKIRYANOVA (AUKHINOVA)

Calculated by current estimates, Marziya lived a short life. Indeed, she hadn't even celebrated her milestone anniversary, which would have been a month or so in the future...

Yet, she left in people's heartfelt memories - not just in those of her relatives' (or those she simply knew and spoke with) - recollections, sweet experiences, and the wisdom gleaned from her earliest years.

Looking back, from the first minutes of our meeting, this woman amazed me with her strength of spirit: her optimism and love of life. Despite the fact she was confined to a wheelchair. Interestingly, people around her didn't seem to notice this device; since she was such an active and cheerful person.

... It all began following a fatal accident on a mountain road in East Kazakhstan. An event splitting her life in twain. Beforehand, Marziya enjoyed a carefree childhood as part of a large family living in the small town of Temir. A place where people went to market in the Aktobe region. She spent happy years as a student in the city of Alma- Ata (bordered by the snow-capped peaks of the Trans-Ili Alatau), bringing up a young family with her partner Kairat. After the accident, however, despair and pain coloured her life to the extent that everyone around her feared the worst. Openly questioning how she could continue living...

Yet, in these darkest of moments, Marziya's relatives were united in their common purpose. They tried to ease both her physical pain and mental suffering. It was very hard for everyone, obviously. Particularly for Marziya herself. Nonetheless, as an extremely active young sportswoman who had tragically became immobilized she realized her spirit remained unbroken.

Defiantly, Marziya gathered her thoughts. After all, her children still needed her care, while her husband required his partner. Certainly, all of his free time was dedicated to her. Attempting, as he continually did, to get her on her feet. Everyone believing in possible miracles, even though nothing paranormal happened. Neither did medical trips to Germany, nor other rehabilitation centers, help above measurable expectations. Instead, it was meeting with casual acquaintances who shared her situation, which proved most effective! Simultaneously, Marziya's physicians changed her thinking about her plight. Each initiative helping her, as well as her family, to approach the problem in new ways.

Excitedly, she learned to walk with the support of splints. This surprised both doctors and patients in her German hospital. Moreover, success followed successes as she learned to jump from the wheelchair into the sea and swim for lengthy periods. No one could have imagined at the time that half of her body was motionless.

On a personal level, Marziya and Kairat had lots of friends. Literally as well as metaphorically, their door never closed. Undoubtedly, wide ranging interests drew like-minded people to them. Lovers of poetry, history, the countryside. Passions they also taught their children. Especially when living in the city of Ust-Kamenogorsk: a basecamp from which they often went on skiing trips, or in summertime, to swim in a mountain river. Occasionally coming to rest near Bukhtarma: a small lake where the whole family built a tiny chalet. Unsurprisingly, Marziya cheered everyone no matter where they were staying.

In herself, she recalled growing up with a loving and caring grandfather and grandmother. As such, according to Kazakh tradition, they considered her their own child. Hence, Marziya learned from them a philosophical attitude to life, how to approach strangers, show kindness, bear responsibility, and other qualities that became distinctive in her personality.

Unquestionably, therefore, Marziya was a highly valued employee wherever she worked – the calculating center for the State Planning Commission in Alma-Ata, for example. Or at the Institute of Software Systems in Novosibirsk. Or for that matter, "EastKazGeology" in Ust-Kamenogorsk. What is more, when she saw how pressured Kairat had become - whole days and nights spent counting (by hand) variants of his theory as a preparation for his dissertations defense - she wrote a program helping him make electronic calculations. Assuredly, productive results soon followed. Indeed, due to her assistance, Kairat proved his theorem. All meaning, in the world of serious mathematics "Zakiryanov's theorem" stands proud.

In equal measure, Marziya was a good friend and assistant in all of his affairs. Thence, when he became Rector of the East-Kazakhstan State University, and prospered in this educational institution, the bad reputation of the "smithy racketeers" it had earned in 1990 slowly vanished. Nowadays, it is the Academy of Sports and Tourism, wherefrom a large number of well-known athletes have achieved global recognition for the Republic of Kazakhstan. Marziya was additionally skilled in relating to those around her. For her daughter-in-law, Svetlana, the wife of her son Baurzhan, along with her son-in-law, Mars – husband to her daughter Asel, sweet Marziya developed into a counsellor. This helps to explain why they all became great supports to their mother and father. Beyond doubt, once they adapted to the new situation; they never upset their parents, but aimed to please them by their successes. Today, Baurzhan Zakiryanov has a PhD and a DBA degree in economics and business administration, whereas Asel Artykova is preparing to defend a doctoral dissertation in the juridical sciences.

Clearly, they gifted Marziya and Kairat with fine grandchildren – Tamerlan, Tomiris, Danat, Arslan and Ruslan.

For her part, Marziya found time to play with grandchildren. To teach them basic values. Thus, it came as no shock to anyone when their first clumsy, childish, but sincere, poems were devoted to her. Their own beloved grandma. In return, she tried to give her grandchildren all the joys of a happy childhood – beginning with toddler's toys, fun books, and eventually, trips to the sea.

As her grandchildren became older, she became their first real friend. Sharing their secrets and dreams with her. Assisting Tamerlan, she studied mathematics: patiently explaining the content of a problem and thinking, along with him, about possible ways to solve it. Marziya even taught him to think systematically. Maybe this contextualizes why he is presently the winner of various mathematical competitions; easily taking science. Concurrently, he, like his grandma, is a romantic: loving poetry and writing in the style of those "Silver Age" poets, so beloved by her. Eventually, as his grandma wanted, Tamerlan was admitted to a College in Cambridge University.

… Personally, she loved Tyutchev poems. In the early days after her accident (once she had returned to herself), Marziya immediately asked for volumes of poetry to be brought to the hospital. One book in particular, a battered brown covered tome, was always with her. Allowing the lines of her favorite poets to resound inside her. Maybe it also reminded Marziya of an inspirational

Russian language teacher named Nadezhda Ivanovna Chupik from her schooldays. A man who inducted her into the mysteries of poetry and classical music. Maybe so! Either way, when she said, "Guys, listen ..." all fell silent: paying attention to enchanted lines read by famous actors, or flinching at the sound of resonant chords. In these moments, Nadezhda Ivanovna flew above her with winged memories. Suddenly, her big blue eyes would fill with tears. Marziya's recollections equally brought to mind that even the most hardened school bully would become quite in the presence of art ..... marking such moments as unusual. Removed from the mundane, but alive to the potencies of rural joy.

... Throughout the 70s, in her small town, there were no televisions. That's why young people often gathered together to play volleyball, football and ride bicycles. Or in the winter, to practice ice skating and skiing. Overall, Marziya knew friendships were made in this manner. Nonetheless, everyone still needed to find time for school lessons, physical training, helping the elderly, working on family farms, reading books, and going out to movies. Thus, she divided housework among younger brothers and sisters like a fair-minded judge. In the evenings, Marziya remembered, her parents would ask her if these instructions had been fulfilled or punishments were due? All confirming this era as a necessary learning curve in her development. Thenceforth, Marziya was a very organized person. A discipline helping her to struggle with her condition long after the accident. So structured, Marziya assisted all those around her, including her children and her husband. Teaching them to put everything in its correct place and to plan their affairs well in advance.

Marziya really loved her little granddaughter Tomiris. Avidly, she tried to discern the features of her character and direct its development towards a positive future. To guide, from childhood, this innocent into the greatest flourishing possible. With these intentions, Marziya taught Tomishko the tricks of cooking. They liked to prepare cakes together, along with cookies and different types of salad. Besides these delights, Marziya told Tomiris how cabbage, tomatoes, as well as herbs, grow. Adding, at the end, their age-old utility. For her part, Tomishko listened attentively to Marziya, eventually presenting delicious meals with her grandma to the entire family. In this, Marziya complimented her granddaughter as a very clever and very capable girl. When people asked Tomishko "What do you want to be?" she answered, "A restaurateur. I want people to enjoy my delicious food! And it should be beautiful!" Transparently, Marziya supported her by saying: "That's right! You will have the most beautiful restaurant! The most delicious food! If it is cooked with love, it will be the most delicious anywhere!" Now, Tomishko really was a very clever girl. Meaning sometimes she had other dreams, However, the foundations laid by her grand-ma continued light up her future life. Similarly, as love received in childhood warms a whole soul – she remains an optimist. When all said and done, such things are extremely important...

Reminiscent of that love which occurs in adolescence and joins one's life to a unique partner, so was the love between Marziya and Kairat. It was a combination of two passions, two strong char-acters, and two emotional spirits! Many around them couldn't un-derstand its nature. Specifically when they could argue with one another over an insignificant matter, not give way to each other and refused to talk for days. Eventually, of course, Kairat would take the first step: "Okay, Honey, I was wrong!" Then, Marziya (be-fore forgiving him) would sort out the controversy in detail, get to the causes of their quarrel, and finally reconcile with Kairat.

A favoured line of Tuytchev poetry reads:

> Love, love - an infusion
> The union of soul with the soul of my darling
> Their compounds, combinations,
> Their merging almost fatal,
> And... a fraught duel...
> Yet, one of them proves tender

In an unequal struggle between two hearts,
That is inevitable and true.
Loving, suffering, sadly numbs,
Until its final languishing …

Together they discussed newspaper articles, political news, all newly published books. Marziya, an unrepentant "owl", often going to bed late: about 1 o'clock in the morning. Nearby their bed was a small lamp used for reading. Yet, Kairat never asked her to turn off the light and usually fell asleep with it on. By morning, over breakfast, Marziya would tell him about the content of the article or book she had read the night before.

When he was very tired and could not sleep, she appeased him saying, "Give me your hand, calm down, everything will be fine. Sleep, I'm near." Then, he fell asleep.

Marziya often quoted these lines of Tyutchev poerty:
Do not argue. Do not hurry! …
Madness looks for stupid judges;
Daytime napping treats a wound,
While tomorrow will be what it will be.

When alive, we can survive all:
Sadness, joy and anxiety.
What do you want? Why grieve?
Another day lived through - thank God!

These lyrical words became ever more pertinent when she struggled with her terrible condition. Every day like an accounting, despite the fact she wanted to achieve great things in this life. To finish writing a book, to plant new seedlings in the garden, to play with her youngest grandson Danat, to discuss family issues with friends, to advise others how to act courageously in difficult situations. And in all these things she succeeded! That year (the one in which she was taken ill), saw Marziya write a book about her predicament "A Life with Pain and Desperation." Furthermore, she prepared for publication a book about her father – "The Road of Life." A front-line diary written by him as a 20-year old boy who experienced all the horrors of war and the delights of poetry. Unsurprisingly, perhaps, its deep philosophical content, uncovered a new side to this man. Sadly, he died too early: which is why she wanted to make sure future generations would be proud of their great-grandfather.

Every day after the physician's consultation, Kairat made sure he supported Marziya in easing her suffering and trying to keep her spirits high. He rejoiced at every moment of improved health, hoping that, eventually, Marziya would triumph over her disability. Alas, this did not happen. Marziya passed away on September 28th, 2013. In her final few minutes, she called to Kairat, and then fell into unconsciousness...

Today, the pain of losing her refuses to abate. But, the trees she planted continue to grow, gymnasiums she founded are working, houses built under her management abound, and her grandchildren thrive, while their dear grandma looks upon them from her tenderly smiling photos...

N. Aukhinova
April 15th, 2015

Being asked to introduce a new collection of poems is always an honour. However, if one is requested to preamble the first-ever assemblage of verses from a Sakha author in our English language - it is tantamount to a gift from destiny's Goddess. After all, such a task is literary history in the making. A magical meeting of cultures, wherein different nations and ethnicities begin to dialogue with one other. Despite, of course, the terms "ethnicity" and "nation" receiving such a mixed press nowadays. A linguistic fact only made comprehensible through the lexical observation that these words mean very different things across the planet. Indeed, for a significant number of Western countries they are simply reactionary epithets. Nostalgic leftovers, so to speak, from a previous age of gross colonial domination. Conversely, in distant Central Asian lands, these concepts are often felt to be the first liberating rays of aesthetic sunshine following the darkness of totalitarian oppression. Almost analogous to the brilliancy shining inside health-giving dew on an early Midsummer morn. Either way, the Sakha poet Kharlampieva seems to take a textual joy from ethno-nationalism as a tacit call for spiritual recovery. In other words, she appears to understand commonplace notions of kith as refreshing articulations of tribal essence against an artificial backdrop of numbing, ideologically enforced, conformity. Strangely reminiscent, therefore, of the tone adopted by Herodotus (484-425), Kharlampieva's poetic works are founded on cults and customs "of the same habits or life". All implying, these traditional bonds unify entire population's jus sanguinis (by the law of blood). Every individual tie encouraging both indigenous creativity and, ironically, an extended cultural tolerance.

Hence, Kharlampieva's corpus is truly unique. Resting, as it does, on a shared Arctic heritage: including a common language, communal faith, and a collective ethnic ancestry - while simultaneously exploring the type of lyrical composition recognisable to humanity in general. So observed, I need to confess a personal (and deeply abiding) fascination with the Sakha Republic. A proud country inhabited by people blending Turkic and Oriental qualities into an overall shamanistic whole. In itself, a further rarefied contribution to worldly ethno-diversity, at the same time as generating subtle and sophisticated insights into our collective species-mentation. Each point taken together, allowing me to unreservedly recommend these brave panegyrics to any English speaking reader genuinely interested in the complexities of Global Text.

David Parry
London 2016

FLOWERS BLOOM ON PERMAFROST
ON THE WORK OF YAKUT POET NATALIA KHARLAMPIEVA.

Few people think about the significance of geography in the fate of any significant poet. Under a bright and hot sun completely different images and metaphors are born than those formed in the freezing cold of -50 C. Indeed, in weather like this, it is even difficult to breathe because of the frosty mist – one ceases to draw breath, while ones lungs refuse to imbibe the icy air. Moreover, the boundless steppes and thick taiga forests generate in the soul of a poet feelings and thoughts that fundamentally differ from those of any poet living in the concrete jungles of modern cities.

So, I guess it seems fair to say that the soul of a poet - no matter how free (by the right of talent) from the shackles of social, or public, life - cannot help but feel the influence, bestowed by birth, of natural habitat and architectural environment.

Therefore, it is no accident that one of the major books by the Yakut poet Natalia Kharlampieva is called "Foremother Asia".

> "It's too hard to grasp
> The depth of my eternal soul..."

Here, as in many of her poems, the key word is "eternity".
Relatedly, the Yakut heroic epic Olonkho was recently translated into English. Originating in ancient times, its roots continue to nourish the growth of modern Yakut literature. Its tone deeply echoing throughout Kharlapieva's corpus. As such, we read:

> «Oh, Foremother Asia!
> Do not break the glorious age's stream
> That I can visit only in my dream,
> Let know all who are capable
> The antiquity of my people,

Do not deny our ancestors,
Whom we recall by restless blood!
Give me, whose homestead is "alas",
That thrill and joy of nexus,
To be the part of a Turkic tribe.

Yet, neither exotic rituals nor ethnographic features constitute the essence of Natalia Kharlampieva's poetry: characterized as these other verses often are by reindeer harnesses, or traditional festivals. No! The main motifs in her poetry are already timeless themes – love and faithfulness, loyalty and betrayal. Indeed, these are the confrontational themes revealing the essence of femininity for Kharlampieva. Motifs of motherhood - not as they are in a household, but in an everlasting sense. Experiences opposed to the brutal, powerful and merciless of men. After all, men frequently want to rule over the whole world. To dominate, dare one say, every individual human soul.

Tellingly, these "feminine" themes prevail in many of her poems and ballads (e.g. "Song of the offended - Kyys Nyurgun"). A composition within which one finds a statement of protest against the absolute power of men over women. All causing some critics to speak of Feminism. If such is the case, this is a form of Feminism alien to the European spirit. Rather, it is a manifestation of those tears wept by a lyrical Heroine. Hence, even in Kharlampeva's romantic poems, there is a thread of historical injustice towards women: to those age-old keepers of the hearth and home. An injustice done to every Mother and Foremother: to each woman (gifted by creation) with an ability to enlighten and predict!

"I'm a fire.
I'm the stars, blazing in the night.
I'm a fire, raging in the wind,
I'm a flame, obedient in the furnace..."

Polar circles, however, as geographical places are haunted by "northern" conceptions of a "permafrost". A frigidity that, fortunately, does not apply to Kharlampieva's work. Instead, within her lines, one feels the heat of a fire – the heat of passion and emotion. So recognized, these are the burning coals of her tribal campfire: warming and giving hope against this permafrost. Certainly, within her warmth the flowers of love and simple human happiness bloom when the Springtime comes. A metaphorical time to which everyone aspires - regardless of their birthplace and residence.

Interestingly, I had a chance to translate Natalia's poems into Russian as early as the mid-1980s. It was exciting to collaborate with her talented poetic texts. Moreover, it was especially interesting for me, since I spent my early childhood in Yakutia: on the shore of the Arctic Ocean – where my father was employed as a Soviet arctic aviator. Even as a child, therefore, I was friendly with Yakut children and their fate. Experiences reignited by Kharlampieva's musings. Looking back, it was as if I had returned to my childhood: an unexpected event allowing me to form a long-term friendship with one of the greatest poets in Moscow, London, or for that matter Yakutia.

> "Want memorable meetings in your life -
> Learn foreign language.
> Immense and great is Pushkin's Russian.
> And English in its strictest style
> Speaks volumes of Shakespeare ..."

Overall, one can only be glad for English poetry readers. Assuredly, they will meet in this book a strong poetic character, who does not forgive gender stereotypes, yet clearly defines the place of a "Foremother Asia" and an "Eternal Femininity". Archytypes not only in the vast expanses of Eurasia, but additionally discovered inside the historical canvas woven by so many of the so-called "small peoples" of the Far North and Siberia. Those far from the historical and cultural map of the entire civilized world.

To conclude, a strong female character in combination with a highly developed lyrical talent is very rare. Comparatively then, Natalia Kharlampieva's verses are like delicate and colourful flowers growing throughout the spring and short summer of her native home - and in the forest, in the desert, and on the tundra. However, they are not growing on blessed and fertile soil, but rather on a thin layer of soil lying on permafrost. On a brief moment of summer in human life, which warms readers with its beauty and love.

Lidiya Grigoryeva
Poet, essayist, photographer
Member of the Union of Russian Writers,
Member of the European Society of Culture, World Academy of Arts
and Culture and International PEN Club, April 2016, London

Poetry offers strong evidence that a nation survives as an ethnic entity. Indeed, while its traditions, culture, and language thrive, a country can still dream of its future. As such, poetry has become an identifier of "ethnic being", or in other words, a group maintaining a sense of self-sufficiency, uniqueness, and a succession of generations. Thus, are the Sakha people!

In Yakut literature, beginning with the poetry of Alexei Kulakovsky and Anempodist Sofronov, the twentieth century witnessed unique examples of poetic skill. Manifesting, as well as preserving, national peculiarities in creative thinking, whilst fundamentally connecting with ancestral lines – ancient Turks. Contrastingly, as a result of close contacts with other cultures across the world over the past three millennia, Yakut literature has also absorbed materials from Global Text without losing its own vital sense of ethnic identity, or originality. A fact proven by Yakut poetry through the inticate weaves within oral folk poetry with clear planetary importance.

So observed, works by women played a significant role in the evolution of Yakut poetry; introducing, as they did, a completely new vision of the world to a masculine one. An insight both gentle and strong at the same time, although awash with potent ethnic emotions.

However, the Women's Muse, which blessed Vera Davydova and Anna Neustroeva in the early 20th century, strangely disappeared for years – allowing their menfolk to create history.

In which case, it was only in the 1970s that a revivifying Yakut literature witnessed the first timid steps of Varvara Potapova and Natalia Kharlampieva. Two authors offering a new poetic illumination to shine with a very special light. Interestingly,

Varvara Potapova was called Kuturgan Kuo (The Lady of Grief), while Natalia Kharlampieva was accused of chanting the fate of a lonely woman who knew only the bitterness of a hopeless love. Yet, each of these poets spread a lyrical understanding and tenderness through their work, along with a delicate aroma of sincere sensuality.

For her part, Varvara Potapova sadly passed away shortly after she had gained notoriety as a poet. A tragic event leaving Natalia Kharlampieva to continue her struggle for a revival in Yakut women's literature nearly alone. A battle, nonetheless, she relished because her creativity inspired a new generation of talented female poets. All establishing, today, Natalia as one of the leading poets of Yakutia. An author whose lyrical voice has become a reflection of our complex age of transformation. Her works, therefore, unendingly enrich Yakut poetry with innovative themes, genres, and verse forms: not to mention an extended poetic vocabulary.

Of course, critical attitudes towards prominent female authors in the early years were largely tepid. For instance, during the 1990s - with its painful dissolution of social foundations and reassessment of spiritual values – it was barely acknowledged that women's poetry (in many respects) became a barometer of cultural adaptation. An omission, ironically, contributing to a needful sense of preservating mother tongue and irriplacable artistic worldviews across this distant region.

Unsurprisingly then, Natalia is the author of over twenty books. Her career beginning with an initial collection of poems Airplane, published in 1976, followed by another eight collections: Anticipating Happiness, The Red Snowdrop, A Clear Night, August, Kumiss of Happiness, Three Verses, The White Cloud, After Ysekh. In 2003 she published a two-volume collection of selected poems and prose. Atop of which, she has published selected rhyming "prose pieces" as a poet. Works including an autobiographical essay «A transparent letter» (2001), a lyrical essay «The Sign of a Loving Heart» (2002), a collection of essays and memoirs «The Other Bank of My Poems» (2007), a popular science book «The Declaration of Love: Yakutia in the Russian poetry of the second half of the twentieth century» and several books of miniatures. Moreover, Kharlampieva's poetic works have been translated into various languages of the Russian peoples as well as abroad. Overall, these Russian translations are presented in three collections: «A Night Flight» (1980), «The Red Snowdrop» (1988), «Koumiss of Happiness» (2004). There is even a separate collection of poems aimed at understanding the genetic roots of the Sakha people - delivered from a philosophical perspective and named «Түүр омук ултүркэйэбин» («I am a fragment of the Turkish people»). What is more, recent years have seen a book «Short Poems», which became a sifnificant genre for the poet («Тоҕус дьоҕус тойук» («Nine Short Toyuk Songs»).

Thus, Natalia Kharlampieva's poetry is equally known for her dramatic attitude towards the world, her elegiac tone, confiding intonation, and confessional style. Argued so, her poetry must be considered a lyrical diary, wherein the poet has recorded her everyday experiences. A technique causing some critics to comment that her work may be perceived as a long poetic novel about a woman's fate, love, disappointment and resentment, finding and losing - as significant milestones within her life. Certainly, based on the titles of her collections, it is possible to determine the storyline of a novel relating to certain stages in the poet's own life, since her poetry is clearly autobiographical in motif.

Observably, the artistic picture of the world created by Natalia Karlampieva has evolved from the subjectivity and intimacy of a lyrical diary into an exploration of deep philosophical questions. A progression compelling serious students of literature to state that in her early career Kharlampieva's poetry was generally perceived as a Romantic verse, whereas now it has acquired a metaphysical nature due to her desire to comprehend the fundamental laws of life around her.

Relatedly, the author has referred to her intonational prose as a logical continuation of her lyrical novels («A Transparent Letter», «The Sign of a Loving Heart», «The Other Bank of My Poems») and so on. Either way, her prose and poetry are created through an application of the same laws of poetic perception, which reflect the poet's self-identity. Offering to readers, as they do, an extremely forthright and honest appraisal of the world and its ways.

All in all, the works of Natalia Harlampieva are crisp and original, even though they relish an abiding traditionalism. A combination that will fascinate international readers who do not have the privilege of speaking Sakha as a language, since everything the poet explores – love, duty, culture, the historical and social roles of women and men, genetic memory ..... along with those people embodying this key to their development – are vital for every person on our planet. Especially those individuals able who to hear the voice of a genuine global wordsmith.

Lidia Romanova, Candidate of Philological Sciences,
Head of the Literature Studies Sector,
Institute for Humanities Research and Indigenous Studies of the
North, Siberian Branch of the Russian Academy of Sciences,
Member of the Writers' Union of Russia.

REVIEWS

"For me, it is very important that Natalia Kharlampieva faithfully preserves a continuity with her teachers, and says many kind words about them. It is a rare thing today, when there has developed a gap - not only in social formations, but also in the traditions of succession. She has inherited a good memory; it links her to the Sakha classical writers Kulakovsky and Oyunsky. In this sense, she is their granddaughter; being in the Upper World, they are proud of her, happy that they had lived, worked, and died for the sake of the Sakha people ..."

Vadim Dementiev, literary critic, researcher, winner of the Great Literature Award of Russia.

"For me, Natalia Kharlampieva is, naturally, a Yakut poet. However, her poetic gift and the civil impulse of her poems allow me to say that she is a poet of an all-Russian level!"

Gennady Ivanov, poet, First Secretary of the Writers' Union of Russia.

"I have been wondering how an author of very modern lyrical works can naturally, and without the slightest effort, plunge into the depths of folk tales, the ancient world of ancestors, and therein breathe while living live within it ... What magical abilities does the poet have that we meekly - although anticipating a new miracle - follow her? Apparently, this is the power of the poetic gift".

Ivan Tertychny, poet, translator, winner of Nikolai Gumilev's Literature Award.

"Whether she writes about love, about friendship, about the fate of her people, or of the entirety of Russia, her words (as if in her hands), hold life. She saves it from a lack of spirituality, hatred, disintegration and chaos, as well as self-destruction ... Happy and rich is the ethnic group that has such people."

Sergei Glovyuk, member of the Union of Writers of Russia, Honorable Member of the Union of Writers of Macedonia, Serbia, and Montenegro.

"Works by Natalia Kharlampieva reflect both an overall vision of the world and her views on art: particularly from the position of a poet and the potential poetic word. She adheres to a traditionalist point of view on the social purpose of literature and the noble, social mission of a poet. Moreover, following the great classical writers of Sakha literature, she tends to emphasize the special role of the Poet as a seeker of truth and as a public servant."

Marina Burtseva, Candidate of Philological Sciences, Senior Lecturer, Institute of Foreign Languages and Regional Studies, M. K. Ammosov North-Eastern Federal University.

In this challenging work, the author raises important social issues, showing herself to be a person of civil position who is nonetheless immersed in the historical reflections and general fate of the Yakut people. Hence, her insistence on the preservation and enhancement of their native intellectual values.

Khadija Asadova
PhD in art, Member of the Union of Artists of Azerbaijan

"Foremother Asia" by Natalia Kharlampieva is a poetry book addressed to her native land and ancestry, to those who lived before her. Moreover, her poems read as a pray for unity among her people: for strength and blessing.

Kanykei Kenensarieva ,
American University of Central Asia
Kyrgyzstan

Poems by Natalia Kharlampieva are like a fine rain falling onto the ground, whereon it becomes water giving life to germinating seeds of kindness, forgiveness, understanding and love ..... "in any country, in any century ..."

Lenifer Mambetova,
Poet and winner of the best female work OEBF-2014
Republic of Crimea, Russian Federation

While in Yakutia, a local legend mesmerized me: afiery Viking warrior sailed up the Lena river to the land of permafrost and melted the heart of an indigenous woman. Their child was the first Yakut; her voice echoes through the ages in Foremother Asia, leaving no one untouched.

Sölvi Fannar Viðarsson, actor, poet, multi-sport athlete,
author of A Poet Trapped in a Caveman's Body and Quis Custodiet
Ipsos Custodes? Iceland

The complexity and depth of content, the perfection and simplicity of form – that's what is the book of poems «Foremother Asia». The author wanted to express the emotions of the modern woman on such abstract things as family, homeland, love, kindness and help in their thinking to find a way to people who haven't found it yet.

Artem Brechko, journalist
Belarus

FOREMOTHER
ASIA

* * *

Through lots of snow and rain,
Soaking wet,
Losing their way and groping,
Wrapped up in ordeals
I've met in the middle world.
Looking for the way
To make my dreams come true,
Turning into the sound
Of my angers and joys,
Being ahead
Of my visions and foresights,
Or leading by the hand
My single straying love -
Three verses have arrived
And I sighed three times...

* * *

When it was so cold
That trees cracked,
When snowstorms
Or blizzards
Swept,
When the heat
Of July
Fell.
Yet, in the middle
Of autumnal rains
Beating down,
My ancestor,
A Sakha man
Would say that in
The force of Mother Nature,
Heating and freezing
Human beings
(Not to knock them down
On evil purpose),
Her nurturing ties were shown
Binding their souls with everything…

* * *

Life is a river,
A great river.
It flows slowly,
Relaxed,
Full of water,
It sends
Calm times
To my fate.
Sometimes
It bobbles
And boils,
And breaks
My quiet bank
With turbulent waves...

Life is a river,
A powerful river.
Even when it floods
It does not cover, or
Wash away
Blindly,
My small island of happiness:
The golden sand of happiness.

Life is a river,
A wise river.
It blesses
Your birth,
Your growth,
Your success,
While accepting
The termination,
Vanishing, and loss,
The death...
Life is a river, a great river,
The force that fascinates!

TRUST YOUR MOTHER TONGUE

To my daughter

You may speak any language:
Speak the Russian of great Pushkin,
Speak the English of Shakespeare
Who everyone kneels to .....
Express yourself in any language –
Climb mountains
To the summits of your thoughts,
Make yourself as clear as you can.
But if you feel like confiding,
Use your mother tongue,
The language of Sakha!
The secrets of your soul,
Intimate feelings,
The joy of happiness,
The sorrow of grief –
They need your mother tongue,
Speak Sakha!
Then the land
Where you were born
Will be always with you,
Through its language
It will bless and protect you.
Trust your love, happiness, truth
To the language of Sakha,
Make your way in life
With your Mother Tongue!

* * *

My grandfather was an Olonkho teller.
He would forget all errands,
Becoming carried away by song and verse
And tell Olonkho.
For several nights
The farmers
Living nearby,
Fascinated by his imaginative flights,
Would listen to stories about
Great warriors
Riding huge horses:
The rise of the evil
And the triumph of the good,
The poor and miserable
Gaining abundant life,
The forgotten stories
Lying at the bottom of ancient times...
My grandfather was an Olonkho teller,
A skinny man,
A misfit.
In everyday life
Still a child
In his heart
He lived
Being admonished -
Called down
By his wife (my grandmother)
Every single day...
My poor grandmother
Must have clawed Grandpa away

Being angry
That her husband was of no use!
She must have been unable
To bear the sight of
Hungry eyes in both children and cattle,
And cold stones of the stove...

Meanwhile Grandfather
Would murmur to himself,
Sitting awkwardly.
Answering - not to the point,
With his thoughts wandering far,
Being there, he was as if absent.
Then, he would have
A puzzled look -
Oh, what an ordeal for Grandma!

Grandfather died early.
Grandma outlived him thirty years
To look after her grandchildren...
Sometimes, she would sigh
And say:
"I wonder why
The evil one
Who ruffled flowing water
And made green branches yellow
Spoke such wicked words?
Why didn't he kick the bucket earlier?
After all, his passion
Never occurred in our kin..."

That was the way she missed her husband.
She knew – as no one should
Not to confuse life with Olonkho.

However, she was mistaken.
While I do not know how and when,
Or whether for better, or for worse,
I inherited his gift of verse.

* * *

A girl looks forward to Ysekh*
While wearing a new dress,
To make a boy gaze after her
And fall in love.

A woman looks forward to Ysekh
To wear new earrings,
To convince other people
That she is happy indeed.

An old woman looks forward to Ysekh
To tie a new kerchief round her head,
To sit at a feast
And recall her past.

Everyone looks forward to Ysekh -
There is no life without Ysekh!

---

*Ysekh – a traditional summer festival for Ladies to worship the gods.

* * *

When I talk to a foreigner,
I see his nature,
His attitude towards life,
However, he praises his values,
I feel I stand toe to toe.
My values are safe,
Since I have behind me
Wise Sakha prophets,
Great Sakha poets,
My father's regard
And the all-seeing eyes of my mother...

* * *

If a poet seeks truth
He will never cling to rulers,
If a poet is a Poet,
He doesn't expect happiness in this life.

* * *

A poet cannot make
Even a worn-out banknote,
A poet cannot save
Even a damaged coin,
He would place his hands in vain
Into a threadbare pocket.
But, a poet does not stand with hat in hand –
He is not a beggar,
A poet pursues no fortune,
He does not need it.
He has a habit,
Of gazing into distant prospects.
With a fate to be poor,
A poet seeks something else.
He produces a different wealth,
To last untold years ahead.

* * *

Someone should take care of someone,
Thus the good spreads.

Someone should teach someone,
Thus, knowledge succeeds.

Someone should worship someone,
Thus, tradition is passed.

Someone should love someone,
Thus, continues life ...

* * *

What is life?
A road to death.
From one turn to another,
From one path to another,
This only road
Leading to death
Has one end only,
There is only one top.
On the last day
When you'll leave this world.
However,
I glorify life.
I will learn
Where this road is leading to.
With dignity and courage
I will continue my journey.
I will climb my final summit
With gratitude.

DIAMOND

In olden days, the Sakha did not like diamonds.
They did not think them precious,
Having found one by accident in a forest,
They did not appreciate it.
For them, the stone seemed to be
Frozen, although human, tears.
And their souls cried -
Scenting a misfortune ...

Now these tears -
Are marvelous jewelry.
And they have no equal in the world.
Yet, avarice and greed
Gnaw into our permafrost,
Since diamonds profit
By being carried away!
But, the anyone who knows
Where this journey leads,
Keeps silent ...

Here comes a round-faced beauty,
Wearing fashionable, beautiful, earrings,
With the tears of our ancestors
Slightly swinging over her tender shoulders ...

* * *

It's me! The way I am,
I have not changed,
I have not listened to evil words,
To malignant gossip.
I have carried burdens
On my shoulders, easily.
I believed, like a child,
The next day will be bright -
It's me!

It's me! I have chosen,
And made my way on my own.
I have seen
Love, life, steadying down,
I have worn as a hat
The love in my heart,
I have walked hand in hand
With my regrets and worries -
It's me!

It's me!
Accept me or not.
I have relied
With power in my words,
Power .....
I am set for a journey
Across the centuries,
Under the rainbow
Of my earthly life –
It's me!

* * *

It is raining in the world –
In Beijing,
Saint Petersburg,
Yakutsk.
The rain is spreading
And stretching
Its transparent scarf,
Patting the passers-by
And travelers
With its wet hands.

It is autumn in the world –
Windy,
Wet,
And chilly.
A golden leaf is flying
Over my summer's joy,
On the edge of my summer's happiness.

The rain is my companion.
The autumn is my friend.

* * *

Shall I set forward
Since I am ill at ease?
Shall I follow the one with the Cross
And find shelter in a monastery?
Or shall I remember I have a drum
And get out the drumstick:
Let my hair down
And start the singing ritual –
It will not fulfill
My earthly life,
It will not come true
In the fate I have chosen...

* * *

All people of the middle world
Believe in something.
All pray to something
As if to gods.

Some pray for the good,
Peace on earth,
Some – to evil gods
Of hostility and envy.

For good people,
Others and life are good.
The ill-disposed
Face grief and sorrow.

I make mistakes and blunder,
However, I hope I'll be able
To carry my faith in Good
Along the way.

*   *   *

I'll recognize a soulmate
At first glance,
As if a bridge will form
Between these eyes of ours.

I'll recognize a soulmate
During small talk,
From the friendly sound
In commonplace words.

I'll recognize a soulmate
And offer my hand.
As light of mutual understanding
Enlightens all spaces around.

People hurry past me,
Cowered as if they are cold…
The fewer soulmates,
The higher value of understanding.

* * *

I was walking through golden rain,
I was walking over golden leaves,
Feeling I knew this life,
I understood that autumn,
I felt I had wings
When I was walking in birch woods.

Then my companion,
Who was walking beside me said:
"Today you are young and beautiful,
The road ahead if wide and straight,
You are in harmony with the world...
Don't you think it's too good to last?"

These unkind words tore my link
With the autumn: with life itself.
Joy vanished in the air - and
I was walking through golden rain,
I was walking over golden leaves,
I was walking slowly,
Lost and sad in birch woods.

* * *

I love my friends!
Loud and courageous men,
Loyal and kind women –
I love my friends.

I love them – thus,
I'll never let
Either slander
Or offense strike them.
I'll even support those friends
Who make mistakes.
I'll give them a hand,
I won't spear good words!
I will be proud
Of my friends
On the days of their glory
And joy.

I always rely on my friends,
So, my love will keep strong!

* * *

This year's April. Thank you
For your tender and caring attitude.
For you are the only guest
In my lonely hut.

Thank you for lovely days,
The nights free of questions,
For teaching my soul
To work and revive.

Sitting here, I have found
The peace of mind that I lost.
I have calmed down. Until my soul
Faces another shock.

AUTUMN RAINS

The autumn rains,
The delayed rains,
They have come
Without a fuss.

The dear land rejoices,
Quietly at peace
In the autumn rains,
So warm.

The autumn rains,
(Steady rains),
Seem to whisper
Of a future to come.

The autumn rain –
Shy and tender,
Is singing a song
Foretelling of joy.

TO THE MEMORY OF MY MOTHER

My mother has died.
The circle of her earthly life
Has completed.
She breathed her last.
Suddenly, unexpectedly, yet early.
My brother and I, the beloved children
Of the one who brought us into this world,
Though grown, have become orphans.

My mother would recall
Uluu Syhyy, where she was born,
With its green meadows,
Far and away,
At the back of beyond,
Where deities
Descended from the sky...
Before the war,
When she was young,
She was there dreaming
Of a good life ahead.
There she tasted
The bitterness of grief,
The sourness of sorrow.
She would tell
That land
Was beautiful: although a bit
Unkind and scary,
With deep lakes,
High mountains,

Yet, full of hospitable spirits.
This mysterious place
With an unusual name
Was the place my mother missed,
Was the youth my mother missed,
Uluu Syhyy, The Great Field,
Where deities
Descended from the sky...

Mother, the breath of autumn
Is not yet felt.
Mother, August
Is not over yet,
Mother, leaves on the trees
Are not yet yellow.
Mother, the heads of crops
Have not grained yet,
Yet you have left
For the land nobody returns from,
For the place where you had come from...

TO MY LORD GRANDSON

-1-

In far Jerusalem,
At the Wailing Wall,
I was standing quiet,
Asking for you above all.

In my home Magan,
In the heat of summer,
I was walking among birch trees
Thinking of your earthly name.

In autumnal Moscow,
During a dark night,
I heard your low crying,
Excited with new joy.

My lord,
My grandson...

-2-

My lord, where did you come from?
From what great heights
Did the supreme ones send you
To make me happy?

What star is shining
To light your way?
What path you will choose
To move along this way?

I held you in my hands,
Soft and warm,
I hope that everything
Will be good in your life.

I will pray to supreme deities,
Sending gratitude!
For my precious offshoot,
For my darling lord...

-3-

My happiness I can hold in my hands,
My precious offshoot, my grandson.
I did not know
You would come that easily.

I did not know that
My life would fill with your smile.
That happiness would come
With the smell of your hair.

I have spread my invisible wings
Over your head.
I have laid my skirt
On the way you walk along.

May you grow and succeed,
My lord grandson, my bird!

* * *

Draw me, my grandson
Through the sky overhead.
With its white sun and stars,
And snow flying late at night.

Draw me, my grandson,
To the crowd at Ysekh*,
The day when souls rejoice,
Summer is glorious - the best!

Please, draw, my darling!
It will fill my heart with power.
I'll sit next to you,
Looking at your life.

Draw me something -
It will illumine the way!

---

*Ysekh - the holiday of summer meeting with koumiss libations.

* * *

If you have never made mistakes,
If you have never been deceived,
Then you have never worshiped the Truth:
You have never paved the right furrow.

If you have never had regrets,
If you have never felt guilt,
Then you have never served the Good:
Have never sacrificed anything.

If you have never loved,
If you have never cried,
Then you have not learned Life:
You may have never lived it, in fact...

* * *

What a great feeling to be free!
From the burden of envy,
From the yearning for wealth,
From the desire of fame,
From the vanities
Of arrogance and pride!
What a great feeling to be free!
Sometimes be stupid,
Sometimes be wise,
To do good for good,
To forgive bad things,
To walk your own way,
To carry what you can!
What a great feeling to be free!

* * *

I am a strong woman
I am Sakha.
Nobody has ever
Paved my way,
Nobody famous
Or powerful
Has ever given me
A walking stick...
A blessing from the sky
Has lit my way...
I made a decision one day
On my own,
I chose my fate
On my own.
I managed to protect myself
From a stupid idea
To rise and become
Great while alive.
Well, I might be naive.
As they say,
Long is my hair,
But short is my wit.
Well, I am just
A common Yakut woman.
I hear everything,
I fell excited and scared
To live as if there was
A punctured wound in my heart,
Dying and coming to life again
One hundred times...

* * *

Having heard the sound,
Having heard the bell,
I will summon four winds
From the four corners into my verse.
My friends since childhood,
My four belts
From all of life's troubles,
Four violent whips,
Four gazes into the distance,
Four wisdoms …
My lips go numb,
But I can bear it.
I'll accomplish all my tasks,
I feel I'm equal to them!
I just need to summon my friends -
The four winds into my verse…

FOREMOTHER ASIA
(a prayer)

When the self-willed blood of my ancestors
Agitates my heart
When I see the way of my people
In the dark starry sky
When the centuries-long nomadic spirit
Awakens in me
When I feel like riding
Clinging to the horse's mane
When I let both joy and sorrow
Enter my heart
I want to kneel
In front of you
And pray in thankfulness!

Foremother Asia!
Before your eyes,
Within your borders
There passed great peoples
The blessed ones
Vanished
The strong ones
Saw defeat!

I am not saying
You treated
My people harshly
Like a heavy stepmother
Or ruled
With iron hands
And made them suffer,
I am not saying

That you hadn't left them
In warm abundant places.
I am grateful,
My great Lady,
For making our thoughts and dreams
Last for centuries
For making strong
Our bones and muscles
For letting us find
The banks of a great river
For hiding us in the depths
Of thick snow
For brining us to the foot
Of magnificent mountains
For preserving
This lifestyle of ours,
For embedding our beliefs in my soul!

Foremother Asia!
Do not cover the past
I see in my dreams at night
Do not hinder
The bright future
Of my people
Do not deny the forecasts
Of my all-seeing ancestors!
Please leave to me,
The girl from a green meadow
A powerful fate rooted in the past
The fortunate strength
Of being Turkic,
The future protected by spirits!
Foremother Asia!
Coupling with your other peoples,

Joining with your other children,
Do not take away our strength.
Preserve our language,
We look so alike.
Do not deprive us of our force,
Do not let to forget our past!
May the blood of those
Who call themselves Sakha run faster
From the soft glance of your eyes
Cast from the bottom of centuries,
From your blessed name,
Glorious, spreading heat!

Foremother Asia!
I am the child
You hid in your wide skirt
I am the offspring
You hold in your warm hands
I am a blessed woman
Who can see far and beyond
I am used to mounting a horse
And riding for days
I have tendons
Heat and frost treated,
I have the bile that can digest
Any ordeal in the present.

Foremother Asia!
With the treasure of your Turkic language
With the means of your Mongol language
With the splendor of your Sakha language
May I speak
May I ask
May I pray!

A ROAD IN STEPPE

The beds of dried-up rivers,
The expanses of bleak steppes,
The sands whispering sadly –
Everything is strange to me.

My soul yearns for
Water, a river or a lake,
Or heavy rain
To saturate the dry soil.

I cannot catch
The winged soul of steppe,
I cannot make out
The yellow spots far away...

My companions are singing
To make the long journey shorter.
The soul of steppe opens
To a smile from a friend.

THE TRIPTYCH ABOUT ANCIENT TURK WOMEN

-1-

In the vast expanses,
Under the hooves of swift horses,
Your names vanished: turned into mist...
Your breast-fed bounty
Against hungry times of enmity,
Which did not feel full and died in a fight...

However, the light of your blessing
Has reached present days
And caressed with its warmth,
It brings us good..

My hair dressed short
Pulls my head back like a thick plait.
The spirit of my ancestors
Has penetrated through my back.
The Turk women's skill and stamina
Has revived in my blood and my looks!

The soul of ancient Turk women
Is my body's secret shadow...

-2-

Oh, my tough elder sisters,
Please share your endurance.
You were the posts that supported
The vast space of the steppe.
You saw your warrior-men
Off to battle,
You sat on the tail
Of the fierce god of war.
You washed blades covered in blood
With your tears.
In the murky darkness
You shed light.
You managed the weight
Of silvery pectoral jewelry.
You coped with
Humiliation from the men -
Please share your endurance!
Oh, my tough elder sisters,
Please share your skill.
You set for the journey far north
Without letting any fire die away.
You thought of throwing Ysekh
To keep our people together.
You walked along with Aan Alakhchyn,
The Goddess of Fertility.
You endured the labour
Of bringing children into this world.
You cleared the back of newborns,
(With Mongolian blue spots), by your tongues –
Please share your skill!

-3-

Due to ancient Turk women's
Strength and skill,
Their good blessing -
Being the offshoots of
Their healthy nature,
Their sovereign beauty -
We must be alive...

"WE ARE BASTARD CHILDREN OF RUSSIA"
Bair Dugarov

We are bastards of Russia.
We - the descendants of ancient tribes.
We do not feel rootless,
We do not consider ourselves orphans.

Along with glory and death
From the depths of the dark ages
Our ancestors ride
On white horses...

The stubborn blood of our ancestors -
Blue Turks and Mongols -
Sometimes trembles
In my temples.

We are bastards of Russia.
The descendants of those who lived in the saddle.
Who loved, gave birth, and died,
In a nomadic, hard, saddle ...

A DREAM IN THE GOBI STEPPE

It is a night in the steppe, Midsummer.
A small bonfire is flaring.
I am sitting by it,
So sad, I don't know why.

I am young. Hopes for happiness
Agitate my innocent heart.
The magic of the word 'love'
Is lighting the space around me.

There have come days
Not to think about love.
A black envy has poisoned
The hearts of my people.

They say it is an old custom
To revenge the people from the other bank.
Sharpening swords,
Making arrows and bows.

Whereas I, last night,
When looking for my foal,
Looked at the other bank
And saw a lad on a white horse.

He was standing on a high bank
For a while, staring at me.
The warmth of his eyes
Made my cheeks blush.

Today sharp arrows
Are cutting the air again.
The evil spirit of death has risen,
The horse, frightened, has vanished.

The lad I saw yesterday,
Placed where your horse took you to,
Why don't the winds blowing form the West
Bring me your name?

So, I am sitting sad at night.
By a small fire
In the Gobi steppe,
In lost times. In my dream.

Swords and spears broke,
Arrows got rotten in the soil.
Times of enmity could not win
The great power of love.

That is why this dream
Has come to me in the Gobi steppe.
The magic of the word 'love'
Has penetrated my soul again.

THE BLUE WOLF

Through the vast steppes,
Between rocky mountains,
Along the paths of ancient Turks
A blue wolf is running.

Passing by treacherous ambushes,
Avoiding dangerous roads,
Through the cruel centuries
A blue wolf is running.

On the outskirts of our Middle World,
Through the strife and quarrels,
Along the path of my freedom
A blue wolf is running.

The blue wolf is running
Through time and centuries,
Reminding us of our ancestors,
The ancient blue Turks...

* * *

It is not troubles that make a person grow old,
Neither does a snow of sorrows.
It is the black ore of blunders
That causes his sleepless nights.

Since each of them – is a betrayal of oneself.
Why send a curse across time?
Each error punches in the solar plexus,
Killing dreams and cutting one's wings.

Without wings, a man burns like a spark.
A wingless man becomes old fast...

OLONKHO AND LIFE
(from the cycle)

-1-

Over dear green meadows
Of our free Middle World,
Cunning devils are galloping
And laughing till they drop.

The gods of the Upper World
Are looking at their roistering: silent,
They seem to know
The fate of our Middle World.

Every day, life erases
The boundaries between good and evil.
It shuffles the deck of destinies,
Not distinguishing between the three worlds...

To modern Tuyaaryma beauty
Hold on a little more, Tuyaaryma!
Believe in yourself.
An Urung Uolan lad
Has never been quick.

His elder brother Nurgun Botur
Is usually late, behind as well,
It is time already.
The brave and glorious warrior is here.

Do not let your craving
Regard with favour
Someone evil and rich
Or accept his gifts!

Darkness gives rise only to darkness,
Scoundrels give birth to scoundrels.
Do you realize that,
Beautiful Tuyaaryma girl?

Do not rush to get away from the Goddess Umsur's eyes.
She will give you advice.
The greatest shamaness sees everything,
She will whisper the answer in a dream.
There are still many
Horned scoundrels in this world.
There are but few honest warriors,
Well, what can one do!

Hold on a little more, Tuyaaryma!

-3-

I feel pity for Soruk Bollur the Messenger of gods!
He rides his path,
Not proud of himself,
Not talking aloud
About his errands.

I peered into him -
Fate is simple, like the palm:
He is on the road again, on the move,
Carrying a decision he's not made.
Yet there is no more important task!

Welcome, Soruk Bollur!
Now, everyone hopes for him:
He may, patting his horse,
Insert his foot in a stirrup,
And catch up with time!

-4-
Oh, my precious warriors!
I wish you enough
Of hope and patience
On your way -
In a battle – victory,
In deeds – success,
In love – an answer!
And may blessing
Win all doubts!

A WOMAN'S MONOLOGUE

I am fire.
I am a star blazing in the night,
I am a bonfire in the wind
And obedient flame in a furnace.

I am fire.
I want to warm and melt
The one appointed to me,
This is my fate.

I am fire.
Do not try to understand me.
My soul is intangible,
Like the spirit of fire.

I can melt ice, if I feel like it,
I can smile at rude words,
I can warm a frozen soul.

If you offend me – I'll wrap you in laughter,
Nothing can make me weaker or reconciled!
I will surrender to one thing only -
The light of your kind smile …

* * *

I often see in my dreams
(I do not know why)
A mare with a foal,
Pasturing on a green meadow.

She is calling her baby to get closer,
She is pricking up her ears, listenin.
The agile foal is running round her,
Then it remembers its mom...

I wake up in the morning,
Feeling guilty, uneasy.
As if I had spied, jealous,
On happiness that is not mine.

RED SNOWDROP

My friend, sensitive and gentle,
Prone to flatter his home land,
Told me about something unseen –
A red snowdrop he had found.

I had never heard about it
Either found in a forest or fields,
About our Sakha nature
Making flashes in spring.

I love my sensitive friend,
Whose soul yearns for beauty.
I know he comes from a land
Where red snowdrops grow cutely.

I see him walking to a meadow
Where I will never be,
His shadow will not be seen soon,
Against those thick forest trees.

There, on a sunny path,
Happiness will embrace him,
The red snowdrop will bloom
Under my window, in the town.

BLESSING

In the ringing frost,
In the ardent heat,
Anywhere,
Any time,
In the dark corners of a winter house,
Under the high dome of a summer dwelling,
In the whirl of an event,
Day and night,
I think about you,
I pray and kneel
Whispering your name...

May the one with evil eyes
Not fix them,
May the one with ill words
Not open his mouth,
May the one with bad ears
Not hear anything,
May the path of success open,
May great days come,
May a shadow never fall upon you,
May worries and regrets never dwell in your heart!
In the ringing frost,
In the ardent heat,
Anywhere,
Any time,
Day and night,
I will think about you,
I will pray and kneel
To your dear name!

A LETTER

"Give up everything and come.
I miss you so much.
Leave your work, let it be –
I am sick at heart."

You'll get my letter. You'll read it.
You'll feel how tired you are.
Your cold fingers
Will feel how cold mine are...

My darling, I hope
I can make you feel happy.
See how I try to put all my warmth
Into yearning words.

* * *

It looks like winter has touched
Two hearts within hours - under its white wing,
In my eyes – the thickest dark of forests,
In my soul – a black moonless night.

Snowstorms, hostile words,
Are howling in my ears.
They seem to take you away
From me, tearing us apart.

I am standing against the wind,
Calling you name and yearning,
I stretch my arms
After you, you are my star.

Indeed, the winter has touched
Us with its white wing,
In my eyes – the thickest dark of forests,
In my soul – a black moonless night.

CONSOLATION

It is a woman's fate –
To wait for Nurgun Botur!
He is bound to come to you,
So wait, he will turn up soon.

Wait - and your belief
Will help you rise above water and fire,
Your tearful eyes
Will invite him from the distance.

Wait until he descends
From the high sky,
Wait until he holds your hand
And enters the house.

Do not sigh,
Tired of waiting,
From ancient times,
Waiting has been a woman's fate.

* * *

Make me blush,
Knock me down with a glance,
Cry out, the whips
Of your words
Or whisper.
Freedom-loving, unbridled,
I would surrender to a small thing –
Your words,
Said to me sincerely
To warn and protect.

A woman should be blushed
By the man she loves.
Without that,
I'll pass
Past you,
Arrogant,
Looking busy,
Without changing my cold glance,
With a wry smile...

Make me blush and stop!

HAPPINESS

How short this word is!
I still don't know what you imply
In this very short,
Yet meaningful word,
What you expect from it...

Meanwhile I hear
In this word
My love for you,
My seeing you,
My fingers running
Through black hair of yours,
My sitting in the warmth
Of your strong arms,
The beating of my heart.

* * *

Do not love the one who doesn't love you.
He would keep looking
Over your shoulder into the distance,
Trying to find a love
He hasn't met yet, but still craves.
The wicked one would just drop by
To get warm at the fire you've made,
He would listen to your words of worship
To gain strength and fade.
Do not love the one who doesn't love you.
You'd be embracing an empty space,
You'd hurt your feet
Over the dried soil, dried grass.
Do not love the one who doesn't love you.
It's like walking in the snow,
Like soaking in the rain,
Your great love turning
Into hard feelings,
While he would keep looking
Over your shoulder into the distance,
As the wicked one would embrace you
And whisper something...

Do not love the one who doesn't love you.

FINALLY, ONE DAY...

Finally, one day,
Bring seven white roses -
Put seven white roses
On the black soil.

Finally, one day,
Think of my heavy burden -
My heavy burden
Nobody has shared.

Finally, one day,
Think how short life is,
How short life is –
Love is not a mistake.

Finally, one day – at a cold stone,
At the cold stone, the black stone,
At the top of the highest
Of seven hills in Magan...

*   *   *

How shall I comfort you,
My yellow leaf,
The summer is over, is over –
My poor orphan.

How shall I entertain you,
My yellow leaf,
The black wing of the rain have covered
My lonely one.

How shall I make you smile,
My yellow leaf,
The autumn with its cold breath has come,
My golden one.

How shall I console you,
My yellow leaf,
The one that is falling, the one that will last,
My fair one.

* * *

I'll keep my words
That weigh
Like a hammer.
I'll hide my words
That are sharp
Like a sword.
I'll give a short answer
To the words of insult.
I'll leave a parable
For my enemies' envy...
And I'll walk away at once
Along roads they don't know,
Over hills they don't see,
So they won't know
How to catch my scent and follow...

SHORT POEMS

* * *

You have taught me
To be silent,
Not to believe
In words.
You have taught me
To be obedient,
To endure
The pain of offence.
You have taught me
To love cautiously,
Not to place hopes
In the future,
You have taught me
To live without happiness...

* * *

Trying to equal a man,
Arguing, competing –
That's what a stupid woman does,
A wise one knows other ways to win...

* * *

Sweet pain – it's love,
Sweet pain – labour and birth,
Sweet pain – the growing of a child,
Sweet pain – a woman's lot,
Her only meaning in this world.

* * *

I think I know life,
I can distinguish black and white,
However, now and then
I make mistakes:
A small one of flattering,
A small one of revenging,
A small one, a tiny one,
Of low betrayal.

* * *

Not my happiness,
But my unhappiness.
Not my wealth,
But my poverty.
Not my fame,
But my sad eyes
Give envious people joy.
When I walk along my life
With my small moments of happiness shining,
Short of wealth yet generous,
Sad in my heart, but cheerful,
Then those people get disappointed,
Their gloomy days get even darker...

* * *

The woods
Have become golden.
The grass in the yard
Has been touched by the frost.
The sky is becoming higher,
Higher and clearer.
The heart is turning more vulnerable
And generous...

АЗИЯ ХОТУН

* * *

Төһө хаары, төһө ардаҕы
Тоҕо кэһэн, бүрүнэн,
Ханан мунан, эргийэн,
Орто дойдуга тиксибит
Ууступ кэммэр сууланан,
Хайа санаам, хайа ырам
Туолар суолун ирдээн,
Ханнык өһүм, ханнык үөрүүм
Дуорааныгар кубулуйан,
Өтө көрүүм, сэрэйиим
Бэриэччитэ буолан,
Биитэр соҕотох тапталым
Мунаах иэйиитин сиэтэн
Үс хоһоон тиийэн кэллэ,
Үс төгүл үөһэ тыынна...

* * *

Мас тоһутталана тоҥор
Тымныытыгар,
Хаарынан көмөр
Силлиэ, буурҕа
Сиксигэр,
Уотунан уматар
От ыйын
Куйааһыгар,
Ардаҕынан таһыйар
Күһүҥҥү өксүөн
Үргүөрүгэр
Мин өбүгэм,
Саха киһитэ
Өйдөөн көрөрө
Самнара сатыыр
Сааллар өһү буолбакка,
Икки атахтааҕы
Буһарар-хатарар
Айылҕа айыы күүһүн,
Кутун-сүрүн иччилиир
Быстыспат ситимин...

* * *

Олох -- өрүс,
Улуу өрүс.
Устар аа-дьуо,
Холкутук,
Үүт тураан
Наҕыл кэмнэри
Мин дьылҕабар
Түстүүр.
Сороҕор сүүрдэр
Балысханнык,
Дохсуннук,
Чуумпу кытылбын
Балкыырдаах баалынан
Сабыта сынньар...

Олох -- өрүс,
Улуу өрүс.
Харса суохтук
Халааннаатар даҕаны
Сотон ылбат,
Тимирдибэт
Дьол дьоҕус арыытын,
Дьол көмүс кумаҕын.

Олох -- өрүс,
Мындыр өрүс.
Төрүүр, үөскүүр,
Киһи буолар
Аналларгын арчылыыр,
Быстар, сүтэр,
Симэлийэр
Өлөр өлүүнү да уйар...
Олох -- өрүс, улуу өрүс,
Умсугутар сүдү күүс!

САХАҤ ТЫЛЫГАР ИТЭҔЭЙЭЭР

Кыыспар

Кэпсэт хайа да тылынан:
Улуу Пушкинныы нууччалаа,
Шекспир тылыгар сүгүрүйэ
Английскайдыы да саҥараар.

Быһаарыс хайа да тылынан -
Дабай сыырдары, хайалары,
Өйүҥ-санааҥ чыпчаалынан
Итэҕэт хайдах кыайаргынан.

Арай иэйэр буолаар дуу
Төрөөбүт төрүт тылгынан,
Сахаҥ сайдам тылынан!
Кутуҥ-сүрүҥ кистэлэҥин,
Тапталын истиҥ иэйиитин,
Дьолун үрдүк өрөгөйүн,
Мунчаарыы муҥкук муҥун
Сахалыы этээр,
Сахалыы иэтээр!

Оччоҕуна эйигинниин
Айбыт айылҕаҥ алгыһа
Аргыстаһыа мэлдьитин,
Ийэ тылыҥ иилии кууһан
Араҥаччылыа, арчылыа.

Тапталгын, дьолгун, кырдьыккын
Сахаҥ тылыгар итэҕэйээр,
Төрөөбүт төрүт тылгынан
Олоҕуҥ суолун солоноор!

* * *

Мин эһэм олоҥхоһут эбитэ үһү.
Кини тугун да быраҕан туран,
Ырыа-хоһоон имэҥэр иирэн
Олоҥхолуура үһү.
Хас да киэһэ
Үлэһит дьон,
Чугас ыаллара
Кини фантазиятын абыгар ылларан
Истэллэрэ үһү.
Айыы бухатыырдарын
Ааттаах сырыыларын,
Хара албын сараланарын,
Үтүө санаа өрөгөйдүүрүн
Баттаммыт-атаҕастаммыт
Байылыат олоххо тиксэрин,
Үтүмэн үйэлэр түгэхтэригэр
Сүппүт тимирбит түгэннэри...
Мин эһэм олоҥхоһут эбитэ үһү.
Күннээҕи олоҕор
Дьаһала суох
Дьарамай киһи
Оҕо сааһыттан иринньэх бэйэтэ
Өрүттүбэккэ,
Эмээхсиниттэн - мин эбэбиттэн
Күн аайы үтүрүллэ,
Күн аайы мөҕүллэ
Олорбута дииллэр...
Оо, эбэм барахсан,
Оҕонньоро туох да туһата суох
Дьарыгыттан кыыһыран,
Бука сулуйан эрдэҕэ эһэбин!
Оҕо да, сүөһү да аччык хараҕын уйбакка,

Көмүлүөк оһохтоох балаҕан
Тымныытын тулуйбакка,
Бука ыксыыра буолуо эмээхсин...
Оҕонньор буолуохсут
Уоһун иһигэр баллыгырыы,
Татымнык тутта,
Сыыһа-халты саҥара,
Санаата ыраах дайа,
Баар эрээри, суох курдук,
Соһуйбут дьүһүннээх сылдьара -
Абаккатын эбэтин!

Оҕонньор өлбүтэ эрдэ.
Эмээхсин сиэннэрин көрбүтэ,
Отучча сыл өссө да олорбута...
Үөһэ тыынара сороҕор
Уонна этэрэ:
«Устар ууну сомоҕолуур,
Күөх лабааны саһардар
Илбистээх тыллааҕы
Били барахсан
Туура тэппэтэҕэ дьиктитин,
Кини киһи ыччатыгар
Салҕамматаҕа хобдоҕун...»

Ол курдук ахтара оҕонньорун.
Билэрэ - ким да хардарбатын,
Олоҥхо олохтон атынын.

* * *

Кыыс кэтэһэр ыһыаҕы
Саҥа таҥас таҥнаары,
Мэник уолан батыһа көрбүтүн
Тапталга кубулутаары.

Дьахтар кэтэһэр ыһыаҕы
Саҥа ытарҕа кэтээри,
Дьоһун дьолун бар дьоҥҥо
Итэҕэтэн ааһаары.

Эмээхсин кэтэһэр ыһыаҕы
Саҥа былаат баанаары,
Түһүлгэҕэ тиийэн олорон
Былыргытын санаары.

Ыһыаҕы кэтэспэт киһи суох -
Ыһыаҕа суох олох суох!

* * *

Атын омук киһитин кытта
Биир үрдэлгэ үктэнэн,
Кини олоҕу ылыныытын
Дьиҥ төрдүн өтө көрөн,
Бэйэ гиэнин өрө тутан
Үгэргэһэр үтүө күммэр
Мин кэннибэр тураллар
Сахам улуу бөлүһүөктэрэ,
Сахам мындыр поэттара,
Аҕам кытаанах көрүүтэ,
Ийэм бүтэйдии сэрэйиитэ...

* * *

Поэт кырдьыксыт буоллаҕына
Былаас кутуругар олорсубат,
Поэт Поэт буоллаҕына
Дьолун бу сиргэ ирдэммэт.

* * *

Поэт соххор солкуобайы
Сонордоһон ылбат,
Поэт кэлтэгэй кэппиэйкэни
Кэччэйэри сатаабат.
Поэт тэстибит сиэбигэр
Илиитин уктар идэлээх,
Поэт ыраах саҕахтары
Одуулаһар оонньуулаах.
Поэт ууммат ытыһын --
Умнаһыкка кубулуйбат,
Поэт барыһы батыһан
Быстахха былдьаммат.
Поэт дьадаҥы дьылҕатыгар
Туох эрэ атын сыдьаайар,
Кэлэр үйэ мындаатыгар
Ураты баайын таһаарар.

* * *

Ким эрэ кими эрэ харыстыахтаах,
Онон үтүө тэнийиэхтээх.

Ким эрэ кими эрэ тупсарыахтаах,
Онон иэйии ситимнэниэхтээх.

Ким эрэ кими эрэ өрө тутуохтаах,
Онон сиэр силигилиэхтээх.

Ким эрэ кими эрэ таптыахтаах
Онон олох салҕаныахтаах...

* * *

Олох диэн тугуй?
Өлүүгэ айан.
Тоҕойтон тоҕойго,
Аартыктан аартыкка,
Биир эрэ түмүккэ,
Биир эрэ үрдүккэ,
Өлүүгэ тириэрдэр
Соҕотох ыллыкка,
Бу сиртэн арахсар
Бүтэһик күҥҥэ.
Ол эрэн, син биир
Олоҕу айхаллыы көрсүөҕүм,
Бу суол ханна
Тиэрдэрин билиэҕим,
Дьоһуннук, холкутук
Айаммын салгыаҕым,
Бүтэһик үрдэлбэр
Алгыстаах тахсыаҕым.

АЛМААС

Күндү тааһы, алмааһы,
Сахалар ахсарбаттара,
Булар даҕаны түгэннэригэр
Улаханҥа уурбаттара.

Харах уутугар холууллара
Ол таас күлүмүрүн,
Оччоттон билэллэрэ
Үтүөнү аҕалымыаҕын.

Харах уутун киэргэл оҥостор
Далбардаах үйэбитигэр
Иҥсэ-обот иҥиэрсийэр
Ирбэт тоҥ сирбитигэр.

Алмаас үөгүлүүр үбүгэр
Ыллсыы харах хатанар,
Саха тиксэр өлүүтүгэр
Билэр киһи сонньуйар.

Кэрэ алмаас киэргэллээх
Саха кыыһа кэлэн ааста,
Саха дьоло, саха соро
Кулгааҕар эйэҥэлээтэ...

* * *

Бу мин! Бэйэм бэйэбинэн,
Кур бэйэм кубулуйбакка
Хара санааҕа итэҕэйбэккэ,
Хоптон-сиптэн самныбакка,
Сүгэһэрбин чэпчэкитик
Санныбар сүгэммин,
Сарсыҥҥы күн үтүөтүгэр
Оҕолуу итэҕэйэммин –
Бу мин!

Бу мин! Бэйэм таламмын
Суолбун соҕотох солономмун
Таптал, олох, түспэтийии
Албастарын билэммин,
Сүрэҕим дуйдаах иэйиитин
Сэлээппэ оҥостон кэтэммин
Кэмсиниини, дьиксиниини
Батыһыннара сиэтэммин –
Бу мин!

Бу мин!
Ылыныҥ, ылынымаҥ,
Иччилээх тылларым
Күүһүгэр уйдаран,
Үйэни уҥуордуур
Айаммар турунан,
Сирдээҕи аналым
Кустугун аннынан –
Бу мин!

* * *

Аан дойдута - ардах.
Пекиҥҥэ,
Питергэ,
Дьокуускайга.
Ардах дьэҥкир былаатын
Чап-чараастык
Тэнитэр,
Инчэҕэй илиитинэн
Айанньыты
Имэрийэр.
Аан дойдута - күһүн.
Тыал,
Силбик,
Сөрүүн.
Көмүс сэбирдэх тэлээрэр
Сайыҥҥы үөрүү үрдүнэн,
Сайыҥҥы дьол кытыытынан.
Мин аргыһым - ардах.
Мин дьүөгэм - күһүн...

* * *

Тэһийбэтим диэммин
Быралгы барыахпын,
Кириэстээҕи батыһаммын
Манастыырга саһыахпын,
Дүҥүрдээхпин билинэн
Былаайахпын хостуохпун,
Баттахпын ыһаммын
Мэнэрийэ туойуохпун --
Ситимнэспэт, силбэспэт
Сирдээҕи олохпор,
Табыллыбат, сатаммат
Талбыт аналбар...

* * *

Сэрэйиэм аймахтыы дууһаны
Биирдэ утары көрүүттэн,
Далапа быраҕан эрэрдии,
Эйэргии көрбүт харахтан.

Сэрэйиэм аймахтыы дууһаны
Кураанах кэпсэтии киэбигэр,
Суолтата суох элэйбит тыллар
Эйэҕэс дорҕоонноругар.

Сэрэйиэм аймахтыы дууһаны,
Илиибин утары уунуом.
Өйдөһүү сырдык иэйиитинэн
Тула өттүбүн сырдатыам.

Тоҥуйдук туттан аттыбынан
Ааһаллар дьоннор ыксаан...
Өйдөһүү сыаната үрдээтэ,
Аймахтыы дууһа аҕыйаата.

* * *

Араҕас ардаҕы быыһынан,
Араҕас көмүһү үрдүнэн,
Олоҕу олус билэрдии,
Күһүнү даҕаны өйдүүрдүү,
Кынаттаах кэриэтэ дайаммын
Чараҥ устун испитим.

Онуоха эппитэ аргыһым,
Тэҥҥэ ипэр аргыһым:
«Эн бүгүн эдэргин, кэрэҕин,
Көнө, кэтит суоллааххын,
Олоҕу кытта эйэлээххин...
Салҕаныа дуо бу мэлдьитин?»

Олохтуун, күһүннүүн тэҥ тыыным
Кыһыл тыл сэтиттэн кэлэйэн
Кый ыраах миигиттэн көппүтэ.
Араҕас ардаҕы быыһынан,
Араҕас көмүһү үрдүнэн
Муммут кэриэтэ бытааннык
Хаампытым чараҥҥа курустук.

* * *

Мин таптыыбын доҕотторбун!
Омун, халыан атарстарбын,
Дьоһун, мааны дьүөгэлэрбин –
Мин таптыыбын доҕотторбун.

Мин таптыыбын – ол иһин
Туран биэриэм суоҕа
Хараардар тылга,
Атаҕастабылга.
Мин мэлдьи көмүскэһиэм
Сыыһар да доҕотторбун,
Мин кинилэри аһыныам,
Көмөлөһүөм,
Күндүлүөм!
Мин киэн туттуом
Кинилэринэн
Өрөгөйдөөх күннэригэр,
Үөрүүлээх кэмнэригэр.

Эрэнэбин доҕотторбор,
Кытаанахпын тапталбар!

* * *

Быйылгы муус устар, баһыыба,
Эн наҕыл, эн холку сыһыаҥҥар,
Соҕотох олорор үүтээммэр
Эн эрэ ыалдьыттаан ааһаргар.

Баһыыба, эн дьоһун күннэргэр,
Ыйытыынан эрийбэт киэһэҕэр,
Дууһа тутуллар үлэтин
Билинэр истиҥ иэйииr эр.

Мин буллум манна олорон
Сүтэрбит олоххо эйэбин.
Уоскуйдум. Дууһам урусхалы
Саҕаттан көрсүөр диэритин.

КҮҺҮҤҤҮ АРДАХТАР

Күһүҥҥү ардахтар,
Хойутаабыт ардахтар
Тыаһа суох үктэнэн,
Бу тиийэн кэллилэр.

Күһүҥҥү ардахха,
Сып-сылаас ардахха
Үөрбүттүү, сир ийэ
Симиктик иһийэр.

Күһүҥҥү ардахтар,
Нап-наҕыл ардахтар
Кэлэр кэм кэскилин
Сипсийэр курдуктар.

Күһүҥҥү ардах -
Килбик, амарах,
Үтүөнү билгэлиир
Ырыалаах эбит дии...

ИЙЭМ КЭРИЭҺИГЭР

Мин ийэм өллө.
Орто дойдуга олоҕун
Судургу эргиирэ ситтэ,
Эмискэ, соһуччу, түргэнник
Сырдык тыына быһынна.
Хааллыбыт биһиги тулаайах,
Сааспытын сиппит уоллаах кыыһа,
Күн сирин булларбыт атаах оҕолоро.

Айыы сатыылаабыт,
Араҕастаах,
Улуу Сыһыы –
Мин ийэм ахтар алаастара,
Хайа эрэ ыраахха,
Атамай түгэҕэр саспыт
Бүтэй сирдэр...
Сэрии иннинэ,
Эдэр эрдэҕинэ
Дьоллоох олоҕу
Кэтэспитэ кини онно,
Аһыы абатын,
Эрэй эгэлгэтин
Амсайбыта кини онно.
Ийэм кэпсээнигэр
Ол дойду
Кэрэтэ киэркэйэрэ,
Куһаҕана, кутталлааҕа,
Чүөмпэтэ дирин̄э,
Хайата үрдүгэ,

Сирэ-дойдута иччилээҕэ,
Илэ биллэр идэлээҕэ...
Ааттыын дьикти
Атын сирдэр
Ийэм ахтар алаастара,
Ийэм ахтар эдэр сааһа –
Айыы сатыылаабыт,
Араҕастаах,
Улуу Сыһыы

Өссө күһүн тыына
Биллэ илик дии, ийээ,
Өссө атырдьах ыйа
Бүтэ илик дии, ийээ,
Өссө хатыҥ лабаата
Саһара илик дии, ийээ,
Өссө бурдук буолакка
Буһа илик дии, ийээ,
Эн буоллар бардыҥ,
Бардыҥ төннүбэт дойдугар,
Айыллыбыт айыыҥ сиригэр...

ТОЙОН СИЭММЭР АНАБЫЛ

-1-

Иерусалим куоракка
Ытабыл эркинигэр
Эн тускун ыралана
Чуумпуран турбутум.

Маҕаным чараҥар
Сайыҥҥы нууралга
Эн сирдээҕи ааккын
Аргыый наардаабытым.

Күһүҥҥү Москва
Хараҥа түүнүгэр
Эн бэбээрбит саҥаҕын
Долгуйа инэриммитим.

Мин тойонум,
Мин сиэним...

-2-

Хантан кэллиҥ, муҥур тойонум,
Хайа үрдүк куйаартан,
Миигин дьоллуур түгэҥҥин,
Үөһээҥҥилэртэн анатан?

Хайа сулус сыдьаайынан
Суолгун сырдатаҕын,
Ханнык аартыгы талаҥҥын
Айанныырга оҥостоҕун?

Сылаас, сымнаҕас ытыспар
Түһэрбитим эйигин,
Этэҥҥэ барыта буоларыгар
Бүтэйдии эрэнэбин.

Үҥэбин үрдүк Айыыларга,
Махтал тылын аныыбын!
Мин көмүс туорааҕым,
Мин кынат тойонум...

-3-

Көтөҕөн ылар мин дьолум,
Көмүс туорааҕым, сиэним,
Бу курдук судургутук
Тиийэн кэлэргин билбэтэҕим.

Билбэтэҕим мин олоҕум
Эн мичээргинэн туолуоҕун,
Эн төбөҕүн сыллаан ылар
Үрдүк үөрүү тосхойуоҕун.

Эн эйгэҥ үрдүнэн
Чараас кынаппын тэниттим,
Эн үктэнэр үрдэлгэр
Киэҥ эҥэрбин тэлгэттим.

Кытаат улаат, чаҕаарый,
Тойон сиэним, чыычааҕым!

* * *

Уруһуйдаа миэхэ, сиэним,
Үрүҥ күнү халлааммар,
Бөдөҥ чаҕыл сулустары,
Намылыйар хаардары.

Уруһуйдаа миэхэ, сиэним,
Саҥа дьылы, харыйаны,
Улахан кыһыл мөһөөччүктээх
Тымныы Моруос оҕонньору.

Уруһуйдаа миэхэ, сиэним,
Ыһыах киэҥ түһүлгэтин,
Үөрүү, алгыс тиксиһэр
Сардаҥалаах сырдык күнүн.

Уруһуйдаа миэхэ, сиэним -
Уйан сүрэҕим манньыйыа,
Олох кэрэтин саҥаттан
Эн көрүүгүнэн ылыныам!

Уруһуйдаа миэхэ, сиэним -
Эбэҥ олоҕу тупсарыаҕын...

* * *

Хаһан да алҕаһаабатах буоллаххына,
Хаһан да албыннаппатах буоллаххына,
Ол аата Кырдьыкка үҥпэтэххин,
Көнө суолу тэлбэтэххин.

Хаһан да кэмсиммэт буоллаххына,
Хаһан да буруйдамматах буоллаххына,
Ол аата Үтүөнү өрө туппатаххын,
Толук тугу да укпатаххын.

Хаһан да таптаабатах буоллаххына,
Хаһан да ытаабатах буоллаххына,
Ол аата Олоҕу билбэккин,
Олорботох да курдуккун...

* * *

Үчүгэйиэн көҥүл буолар!
Көҥүл буолар ымсыыттан,
Үрдүк солоҕо тардыһыыттан,
Бөлүһүөк аатырар баҕаттан,
Бэйэни киэпкэ симинэр
Улуутумсуйууттан!
Үчүгэйиэн көҥүл буолар,
Акаарытык тыллаһар,
Сороҕор син өйдөөҕүмсүйэр,
Эйэҕэ эйэнэн эргийэр,
Өскө өһү өһүлэр,
Бэйэҥ ыыргынан сылдьарыҥ,
Бэйэҥ сүгэһэргин сүгэриҥ!
Үчүгэйиэн көҥүл буолар...

* * *

Ааттаах-суоллаах аймах бэрдэ
Суолбун тэлэн биэрбэтэҕэ,
Бэйэм эрэлим, санаам күүһэ
Олохпор сирдээбитэ.

Дьонтон ордук мындыр өйдөөх
Дэнэргэ ымсыырбатаҕым,
Тыыннаах сылдьан улуу буолар
Аналга таласпатаҕым.

Аспынааҕар кылгас өйдөөх
Кэнэн саха дьахтарабын,
Ороммуттан оһохпор
Тиэстэр кылгас орохпор
Сүүс санааҕа ылларабын,
Сүүстэ өлөн ылабын,
Сүүстэ тиллэн кэлэбин...

Ол да иһин дьиксинэ
Тулабын көрүнэбин,
Дьон көрбөтүн көрөбүн --
Бэрт былдьаһыы былаҕайыгар
Кэлэр кэскил былдьанарын,
Бөлүһүөгэ суох үйэбэр
Омугум бытанарын...

* * *

Бэйэм билэр тыалларбын,
Түөрт курбуу курдарбын,
Түөрт сытыы кымньыыбын,
Түөрт көрүүбүн,
Түөрт билиибин
Ыҥыран эрэ ылларбын
Барыта илиим иһигэр,
Барыта санаам хоту,
Ырам хоту,
Баҕам хоту!

Бэйэм билэр тыалларбын
Ыҥыран эрэ ылларбын...

АЗИЯ ХОТУН
(ааттал)

Өбүгэм хаҥыл хаана
Сүрэхпин хамсаттаҕына,
Сулустаах хара халлааҥҥа
Омугум суола көһүннэҕинэ,
Үйэлэри нөҥүөлээбит
Көс санаам уһугуннаҕына,
Ат сиэлигэр сыста сүүрдэр
Баҕа санаам дьалкыйдаҕына,
Дьолу, сору тэбис-тэҥҥэ
Иҥиэттэ иҥэриннэхпинэ,
Эн иннигэр тобуктуу түһэн
Анал тылларбын -
Амалыйыахпын баҕарабын!

Оо, Азия хотун!
Эн хараҕыҥ далыгар,
Эн эйгэҥ иитигэр
Улуулар да уостубуттара,
Саргылаахтар да
Самныбыттара,
Күүстээхтэр да
Күрдьүллүбүттэрэ!

Мин омукпун
Тоҥкуруун хааннаах
Маачаха ийэлии
Кытаанахтык тутан,
Хабырдык дьаһайан
Иэдэппитиҥ диэбэппин,
Ичигэс сирдэргэ,
Киэҥ кэйээр киэлитигэр
Күөмчүлүү күөйэн
Кистээбэтэҕиҥ диэбэппин.
Махтанабын эйиэхэ,
Улуу-дьаалы хотунум,
Өйүм-санаам ситимин
Үйэлэргэ салҕаабыккар,
Этим-хааным чиргэлин
Хаҕыстык хатарбыккар,
Улуу эбэ эҥэрдэрин
Булларбыккар,
Халыҥ хаардар
Хоннохторугар хорҕоппуккар,
Хаарыан хайалар
Тэллэхтэригэр тиэрдибиккэр,
Олохпут оҥоһуутун
Ордорон биэрбиккэр,
Итэҕэлбит тутулун куппар иҥэрбиккэр!

Оо, Азия хотун!
Түүлбэр көстөр
Түҥ былыргыбын үрэйимэ,
Омугум салҕанар
Сырдык сабаҕалааһыммын
Сахсатыма,
Бүтэйдии сэрэйэр
Дьоһун өбүгэлэрбин мэлдьэһимэ,
Хааллар миэхэ, алаас
Маанылаах кыыһыгар,
Үйэлэртэн кэлбит улуу ситиммин,
Түүр омук сорҕотобун дэнэр
Дьоллоох добуммун,
Сахтарга салҕанар иччилээх сыдьааммын!

Оо, Азия хотун!
Кыраларгар кыттыһыннараҥҥын,
Аччыгыйдаргар ханыылааҥҥын,
Көмүс күүспүтүн өһүлтэримэ,
Тылбытынан таҥаҥҥын,
Дьүһүммүтүнэн дьүөрэлээҥҥин
Сүдү кыахпытын кыаһалатыма,
Түҥ былыргыбытын умуннарыма!
Сахабын дэнээччи хаана хамсаатын
Үйэлэр түгэхтэриттэн одууһалар
Сымнаҕас харахтаргыттан
Биллэн ааһар, итиинэн илгийэр
Алгыстаах аккыттан!

Оо, Азия хотун!
Киэҥ энэргэр кистээбит
Оҕоҥ буолабын,
Уһуну-киэҥи ырыҥалыыр
Уйгулаах ураанхайбын,
Ат үрдщүгэр ыстана үөрүйэх
Уһунньут айанньыппын,
Куйааһы, тымныыны инэриммит
Инчэҕэй инэиирдээхпин,
Аныгы кэм албаһын өһүлэр
Өлбөт үөстээхпин...

Оо, Азия хотун!
Анаар дуу алгыскын өссө төгүл,
Көр дуу эргиллэн
кыламаныҥ быыһынан,
Мичээр дуу сайаҕастык саннын үрдүнэн!

Оо, Азия хотун!
Түүр тылыҥ үлтүркэйинэн,
Моҕол тылыҥ модунунан,
Саханҥ тылын сарбынньаҕынан
Саҥардаҕым буоллун,
Көрдөстөҕүм буоллун,
Ааттастаҕым буоллун!

ИСТИЭПКЭ АЙАН

Уолбут үрэхтэр омооннора,
Кураанах истиэп нэлэмэнэ,
Кумах курус сипсигэ --
Барыта дьикти миэхэ.

Ууга, күөлгэ, үрэххэ
Дууһам баһарар кубулуйуон,
Эбэтэр дохсун ардаһынан
Хаппыт буорга тохтуон.

Истиэп кынаттаах кута
Миэхэ букатын ситтэрбэт,
Саһахтарга туох саһара
Харахпар таба туттарбат...

Уһун айаны кылгатаары
Аргыстарым ыллыыллар.
Доҕор истиҥ мичээригэр
Истиэп дууһата арыллар.

БЫЛЫРГЫ ТҮҮР ДЬАХТАЛЛАРЫН ТУҺУНАН ТРИПТИХ

-1-

Эһиги ааккыт киэҥ кэйээргэ
Ахсым аттар туйахтарын анныгар
Сүппүтэ, уостубута, күдэн буолбута...
Эһиги ыанньыйбыт эмиийгитин
Кыргыс кэмэ иҥсэлээхтик эммитэ,
Топпута көстүбэккэ охсуһууга охтубута...

Арай, алгыскыт аламаҕай сырдыга
Бүгүҥҥү күҥҥэ тиийэн кэлбитэ,
Сылааһынан сыдьаайа,
Үтүөнэн үөдүйэ...

Мин кыргыллыбыт кылгас баттаҕым
Суон суһуох курдук тиэрэ тардар,
Былыргы өбүгэм үтүөкэн илдьитэ
Сүнньүбүнэн тэбэ кэйэн киирэр,
Түүр дьахтарын мындыра, тулуура
Хаҥыл хааммар, майгыбар тиллэр!

Былыргы түүр дьахтарын кута -
Мин бодом кистэлэҥ күлүгэ...

-2-

Оо, тыйыс эдьиийдэриэм,
Бэрсиҥ даа, тулуургутуттан,
Нэлэмэн истиэп, киэҥ куйаар
Туллар тутааҕа буолбуттар,
Эр киһини, боотуру
Кыргыһыыга атаарбыттар,
Сэрии сэлиик илбиһин
Кутуругар олорсубуттар,
Хааннаах хара батыйаны
Харах уутунан сайҕаабыттар,
Им балай хараҥаҕа
Сырдык сыдьаайы сахпыттар,
Илин кэбиһэр, кэлин кэбиһэр –
Ыйааһынын уйбуттар,
Тойон эр атаҕастабылын
Умса көрө ылыммыттар –
Тулуургутуттан бэрсиҥ!

Оо, тыйыс эдьиийдэриэм,
Бэрсиҥ даа, мындыргытыттан,
Аал уоту умулларбакка
Тус хоту айаҥҥа турбуттар,
Айыы аймаҕа тэйбэтин диэн
Ыһыах туһун санаабыттар,
Аан Алахчын Айыыһыты
Батыһыннара хаампыттар,
Үс саха үксүүрүгэр
Талыы таһыырын тулуйбуттар,
Кыһыл оҕо мэҥнээх сиһин
Ымманыйа сыллаабыттар –
Мындыргытыттан бэрсиҥ!

-3-

Былыргы түүр дьахталларын
Дьоһун, мындыр дьаһалларын,
Алгыстаах сырдык санааларын,
Чэгиэн, толуу бэйэлэрин,
Кэрэ, мааны сэбэрэлэрин,
Сыдьааннара буоламмыт
Сырыттахпыт эбитэ дуу...

ГОБИ ИСТИЭБЭР ТҮҮЛ

Түүҥҥү истиэп. Сай ортото.
Симик кутаа умайар.
Олоробун ол уот аттыгар
Туохтан эрэ олус мунчааран.

Мин эдэрбин. Туҥуй сүрэхпин
Үөрүү сибикитэ долгутар,
Таптал диэн тыл абылаҥа
Тулабын дьиктитик сырдатар.

О, таптал туһунан саныырга
Табыгаһа суох күннэр үүммүттэр,
Хара өс илбиһэ бар дьоммун
Харааччы булкуйбут, иирдибит.

Өрүс уҥуоргу көс дьонтон
Иэстэһэр сылтахтаах үһүбүт,
Өстөһүү батаһа сытыыланар,
Өргөс-кылаан сүлүһүннэнэр.

Оттон мин бэҕэһээ киэһэ
Кулунчукпун көрдүү сылдьан,
Көрбүтүм анараа кытылга
Үрүҥ аттаах уоланы.

Кини миигин одуулаһан
Томторго балай да турбута,
Хараҕын уотун сылааһа
Мин иэдэспин итиппитэ...

Бүгүн эмиэ сытыы охтор
Салгыны хайыта сүүрдүлэр,
Өлүү хаан иччитэ саһыгыраата,
Сиргэммит ат тыбыырда, кистээтэ.

Бэҕэһээ көрбүт уоланым,
Ханна тиийдэ эн үрүҥ атыҥ,
Арҕааттан үрэр тыаллар
Ааккын тоҕо ааттаабаттар?

Түүҥҥү хараҥаҕа муҥатыйа
Симик кутаа аттыгар
Олоробун сүппүт үйэҕэ
Гоби истиэбэр. Түүлбэр.

Батас, үҥүү үлтүрүйбүт,
Охтор сытыйбыттар буорга.
Арай таптал сүдү күүһүн
Кыайбатах кыргыс үйэтэ.

Ол иһин Гоби истиэбэр
Ити түүл миэхэ кэллэҕэ,
Таптал диэн тыл абылаҥын
Саҥалыы дууһабар куттаҕа.

МЫ ВНЕБРАЧНЫЕ ДЕТИ РОССИИ...

Баир Дугаров,
Бурятия норуодунай поэта.

Россия булумньу оҕолоро -
Былыргы омуктар сорҕолоро...
Төрдө-ууһа суох тулаайахтыы
Санаммаппыт биһиги чахчы.

Үтүмэн үйэлэр түгэхтэригэр
Өбүгэбит үрүҥ атынан көтүтэр,
Бэйэни билинэр кыахпытын
Ол көстүү тилиннэрэр.

Күөх түүрдэр, моҕоллор
Хаҥыл хааннарын дуораана
Бүгүн да чараас чабырҕайбар
Тиҥиргэччи тэбэн кэлэр.

Ат үрдүгэр төрүүр, өлөр
Тыйыс аналлаах норуоттар
Ыһыллыбыт сыдьааннара -
Россия булумньу оҕолоро...

КҮӨХ БӨРӨ

Киэҥ кэйээр киэлитинэн,
Үрдүк хайалар быыстарынан,
Улуу түүрдэр ырдарынан
Күөх бөрө сүүрэр.

Үтүмэн үйэлэри нөҥүөлээн,
Сүүс тоһууру быһалаан,
Тоҕус моһолу туораан
Күөх бөрө сүүрэр.

Орто туруу дойдубар
Мөккүөр, киирсии эйгэтигэр,
Мин көҥүл санаабар
Күөх бөрө сүүрэр.

Күөх бөрө сүүрэр, сүүрэр,
Күөх түүрдэри өйдөтөр,
Хантан хааннаах, кимтэн кииннээх
Эбиппитин санатар...

* * *

Киһи кырдьар тапталтан,
Дьоллуур, сордуур абытайтан,
Нөҥө-маҥаа иэйиилэртэн,
Быстах, тутах эйэргэһииттэн.

Киһи кырдьар үлэттэн,
Үөрдэр, хомотор түбүктэн,
Бэрт былдьаһыыттан, ымсыыттан,
Сыыһа-халты дьаһалтан.

Киһи кырдьар төрүөҕүттэн
Син биир төннөр аналтан
Мүччү түспэт иэдээнтэн...

ОЛОҤХО УОННА ОЛОХ
(циклтэн)

Орто туруу бараан дойдум
Алгыстаах алаастарынан
Адьарай оҕолоро
Алларастыы сырсаллар.

Көхсүттэн тэһииннээх
Күн айыы дьоммун
Үөһээҥҥи Айыылар
Атыҥырыы көрөллөр.

Олох обургу күннэтэ
Үс эйгэ быыһын суурайар,
Үс таһым бүтэйин үрэйэр,
Үс аҥыы аналы бутуйар...

Аныгы кэм Туйаарыматыгар

Туйаарыма, тулуктас!
Эрэн бэйэҕэр эрэ.
Сыылба, бытаан Үрүҥ Уолан
Кэлиэ эрэ, кэлимиэ эрэ.

Улахан убайыҥ Ньургун Боотур
Тоҕо эрэ тардылынна,
Хорсун, хоодуот бэйэтэ
Бытаара айгыһынна.

Адьарай уолун албаһыгар,
Кини баайыгар, көмүһүгэр
Ымсыырбатыҥ буоллар дуу,
Дураһыйбатыҥ буоллар дуу!

Сидьиҥ сидьиҥи төрөтөр,
Хараҥа хараҥаны үөскэтэр,
Ону сатаан араарар
Кыыскын буолбаат, Туйаарыма?

Айыы Умсуур удаҕан
Хараҕын далыттан тахсыма,
Түүлгэр биэрэр сүбэтин
Бука диэн, быһа гыныма…

Күн сирин күндэлэс олоҕор
Адьарайдар субу бааллар,
Сиэрдээх, хоһуун боотурдар
Улам аҕыйаан иһэллэр…

Туйаарыма, тулуктас!
Сорук-боллуру аһынабын.
Үтүөмсүйэ барбакка,
Тупсарына сатаабакка,
Хайдах баарынан
Бэйэтин ыырынан
Айаннаахтыыр.

Сорук Боллуру сэргиибин.
Судургу аналлааҕы,
Илдьит иччилээҕи,
Сиргэ тирэхтээҕи,
Олоххо баҕалааҕы!

Сорук Боллуру ордоробун -
Кэм-кэрдии ыгым тэтимин
Кини эрэ уйар курдук,
Кини эрэ ситэр куруук...

* * *

Оо, кырдьыксыт боотурдарыам!
Аан дойду олоҕун очурун
Көннөрөр туһугар,
Алгыс кырыыска хаһан да
Кыайтарбатын туһугар,
Айаҥҥа -- эрэллээх,
Суолга -- тулуурдаах,
Түбүккэ - ситиһиилээх,
Охсуһууга -- кыайыылаах,
Тапталга -- дьоллоох
Буолларгыт даа!

ДЬАХТАР САНААТА

Мин - уоппун.
Сулуспун хараҥа халлааҥҥа,
Кутаабын тыа саҕатыгар,
Дьиэтийбит оһох төлөнөбүн.

Мин - уоппун.
Сылытар, ириэрэр баҕалаахпын,
Ыраахтан ыҥырар аптаахпын,
Айылҕаттан оннук аналлаахпын.

Мин - уоппун.
Санаабын табарыҥ уустук,
Син биир уот иччитинии
Дууһам кубулҕат, хараҥа.

Баҕарыам - тоҥу уулларыам,
Холус тылы мичээргэ кубулутуом,
Тоҥуй дууһаны иччилиэм.

Хомотуоҥ - күлүнэн бүрүнүөм
Уонна биир эрэ албаска бэриниэм -
Эн эрэ мичээриҥ сыдьаайыгар.

* * *

Сотору-сотору түһүүбүн
(Тоҕо эбитэ буолла?)
Төгүрүк алааска мэччийэр
Кулунчуктаах биэни.

Оҕотун ыҥыран иҥиэттэр,
Иһиллиир кулгааҕын чөрөтөн.
Мэник кулунчук тула көтөр,
Эмэр ийэтин, өйдөөн кэлэн...

Туора дьон дьолун
Уоран көрбүт кэриэтэ,
Ымсыыран-буруйданан
Уһуктабын сарсыарда.

КЫҺЫЛ НЬУРГУҺУН

Мин омун, мин нарын доҕорум
Дойдутун киэргэтэр уоҕар
Кэпсээбитэ ким да билбэтин --
Кыһыл ньургуһуну булбутун.

Ханнык да сыһыыга, кырдалга
Истибэтим ол оннук баарын,
Сахам сирин тыйыс айылҕата
Сааскыттан чаҕылын ыспытын.

Кэрэҕэ тардыһар дууһалаах
Мин омун доҕорбун таптыыбын,
Кырдалыгар кыһыл ньургуһуннаах
Дойдуттан кэлбитин билэбин.

Билэбин мин хаһан да тиксибэт
Алааспар айаннаан иһэрин,
Бүгүн дуу, сарсын дуу күлүгэ
Хара тыа кэтэҕэр сүтүөҕүн.

Ол онно күннээх ыллыкка
Дьол кинини кууһуоҕа.
Мин түннүгүм анныгар
Кыһыл ньургуһун тыллыаҕа.

АЛГЫС

Бытарҕан тымныыга,
Өҥүрүк куйааска,
Хайа да дойдуга,
Хайа да үйэҕэ,
Тоҥ балаҕан чэҥнээх муннугар,
Сырдык ураһа үөлэһин анныгар,
Аныгы кэмим бутуурун быыһыгар
Түүннэри-күннэри
Эн тускун саныыбын,
Эн сырдык ааккар
Үҥэбин, сүктэбин...
Кырыылаах харах
Кынчыатыы көрбөтүн,
Уодаһыннаах тыллаах
Уоһун өһүлбэтин,
Дьүлэй кулгаахтаах
Чуҥнуу сатаабатын,
Кыайыы суола аһыллан биэрдин,
Өрөгөй күнэ үүнэн кэллин,
Эн үтүө ааккар күлүк түспэтин,
Эн тойон сүрэххэр хом санаа хоммотун!
Бытарҕан тымныыга,
Өҥүрүк куйааска,
Хайа да дойдуга,
Хайа да үйэҕэ
Түүннэри-күннэри
Эн тускун саныахпын,
Эн сырдык ааккар
Үҥүөхпүн, сүктүөхпүн!

СУРУК

«Барытын бырах, кэлэ тарт.
Ахтан аҥарым хаалла.
Буолар буоллун. Үлэ хааллын -
Санаам олус ыараата».

Сурукпун тутуоҥ. Ылан ааҕыаҥ.
Сылайбытыҥ дьэ биллиэ.
Эн тоҥмут тарбахтаргын
Тымныы санаа хаарыйыа...

Доҕоруом, хайдах гынан
Мин Эйигин үөрдэбин...
Хайдах ахтылҕан кынатын
Итии, нарын тыынныыбын?

* * *

Кыһын тымныы кынатынан, арааһа,
Эн биһикки сүрэхпитин хаарыйбыт,
Харахпар - хара тыа санньыара,
Дууһабар - ый быыһа хараҥа.

Бууртьалар, өһүөн тыллар
Ыйылыы ытыыллар кулгаахпар,
Эйигин, миигиттэн туоратан,
Илдьэ барбыт курдуктар.

Батыһа, хаһыытыы, сайыһа
Тыалы утары турабын,
Илиибин уунабын Эйиэхэ,
Ааспыт сулуспун аһыйа.

Кырдьык, кыһын тымныы кынатынан
Эн биһиккини хаарыйбыт эбит дии,
Харахпар - хара тыа санньыара,
Дууһабар - ый быыһа хараҥа...

УОСКУТУУ

Дьахтар киһи анала -
Кэтэс Ньургун Боотуру!
Кэлиэхтээх кини эйиэхэ,
Күүт, кэлиэ сотору...

Күүт, эн итэҕэлиҥ
Ууттан, уоттан таһаарыа,
Ытамныйбыт хараҕыҥ
Ыраахтан үтүөҕэ ыҥырыа.

Күүт, үрдүк халлаантан
Хаһан көтөн кэлэрин.
Күүт, дьиэ таһыттан
Уолун сиэтэн киирэрин.

Кэтэһэртэн сылайан
Үөһэ тыыныма эн,
Күүтүү - дьахтар анала
Былыыр-былыргыттан.

* * *

Кыбыһыннар миигин,
Батары көрөн самнар,
Кымньыы курдук тылларгын
Хаһыытаа,
Биитэр сибигинэй.
Көнүл, ханыл бэйэм
Бэриниэм этэ бэрт кыраһа --
Кытаанахтык,
Мин туспар этиллибит
Буойар, харыстыыр тылларгар!

Дьахтар кыбыстыах тустаах
Таптыыр эр киһититтэн.
Онто суох ааһыам,
Ааһыам аттыгынан
Өйдөөбүмсүйэ,
Боччумура,
Тоҥуй дьүһүммүн ыһыктыбакка,
Үгэргиирбин кистээбэккэ...

Кыбыһыннар миигин!

ДЬОЛ

Кылгас да тыл!
Билбэтим Эн тугу кистииргин
Ити иччилээх, имэҥнээх
Кып-кылгас тылга,
Тугу эрэнэ кини кэтэҕэр угаргын...

Оттон мин билигин
Бу тылга истэбин
Эйигин таптыыры,
Эйигин көрөрү,
Эн хара баттаххар
Тарбаҕым дайарын,
Эн илииҥ эрчимнээх иитигэр
Чуумпуран олорон
Сүрэхпин истэрбин.

* * *

Таптаама эйигин таптаабаты.
Син биир кини көрүө үрдүгүнэн,
Үрдүгүнэн ырааҕы одуулаһыа,
Тиксибэтэх такталын
Кэтии, көрдүү сылдьыа.
Эн умайар уотуҥ төлөнүгэр
Аат харата сыстан ылыа,
Эн ааттаһар алгыстаргар
Аара иттэн эрэ ааһыа.
Таптаама эйигин таптаабаты.
Кураанаҕы мэлдьи кууһуоҥ,
Куурбут буорга, хаппыт окко
Атахтаргын быһа сынньыаҥ
Таптаама эйигин таптаабаты.
Хаарга хаамыаҥ,
Сииккэ сиэлиэҥ,
Айбыт улуу такталгыттан
Абаккарыы эрэ хаалыа,
Кини буоллар үрдүгүнэн,
Үрдүгүнэн көрө сылдьыа,
Аат харата кууһан ылан
Тугу эрэ сибигинэйиэ...

Таптаама эйигин таптаабаты!

СААТАР ОННО

Саатар онно аҕалаар
Сэттэ маҥан розаны,
Сэттэ маҥан розаны
Хара буорга эн уураар.

Саатар онно эн санаар
Дьылҕам уустук тардыытын,
Дьылҕам уустук тардыытын
Ким да өһүлбэтэҕин.

Саатар онно эн өйдөөр
Олох барахсан кылгаһын,
Олох барахсан кылгаһын –
Таптыырга буруй суоҕун.

Саатар онно -- тымныы тааска,
Тымныы тааска, хара тааска,
Маҥан үрдүк хайатыгар,
Сэттэ сэмэ үрдүгэр...

* * *

Тугунан эйигин уоскутабын,
Араҕас сэбирдэҕим,
Сайын бүттэ, сайын бүттэ -
Мин тулаайахчааным.

Тугунан эйигин аралдьытабын,
Араҕас сэбирдэҕим,
Ардах сапта хара кынатынан,
Мин соҕотохчоонум.

Тугунан эйигин алы гынабын,
Арадас сэбирдэҕим,
Курус тыыннаах күһүн кэллэ,
Мин көмүсчээним.

Тугунан эйигин саататабын,
Араҕас сэбирдэҕим,
Кэхтии кэмнээх, алгыс үйэлээх,
Мин сырдыкчааным...

* * *

Сүүскэ биэрэр сүлүгэс тылы
хаһааннаҕым буоллун,
Айахха анньар уһуктаах тылы
ууруннаҕым буоллун!
Атаҕастабыллаах этиилэргэ
ханарытан эппиэттиэххэ,
Өһүөнү иитэр өстөөххө
үгэргээһини бэлэхтиэххэ...
Уонна холкутук, дьоһуннук
оргууй тахсан барыахха
Кинилэр сиппэт суолларынан,
Кинилэр билбэт үрдэллэринэн,
Хаһан таба өйдөнөөрү,
Хаһан кэлэн өйдөһөөрү...

КЫЛГАС ХОҺООННОР

* * *

Эн миигин үөрэттиҥ
Саҥата суох буоларга,
Тылынан мэктиэни
Ахсарбакка.
Эн миигин үөрэттиҥ
Истигэн буоларга,
Атаҕастабыл абатын
Уйарга.
Эн миигин үөрэттиҥ
Сэрэхтик таптыырга,
Кэлэр кэскилгэ
Эрэммэккэ.
Эн миигин үөрэттиҥ
Дьоло суох буоларга...

* * *

Эр киһилиин тэҥнэһэр,
Мөккүһэр, бэрт былдьаһар
Акаары дьахтар дьаллыга.
Өйдөөх атыннык кыайыаҕа...

* * *

Минньигэс абытай - таптал сайына,
Минньигэс абытай - талыы киириитэ,
Минньигэс абытай - оҕо улаатыыта,
Минньигэс абытай - дьахтар дьылҕата,
Кини олоҕун соҕотох суолтата.

* * *

Олоҕу билэбин дэнэбин,
Үрүҥү-хараны араарабын.
Ол да буоллар ардыгар
Син биир киирэн биэрэбин.
Кырачаан тургутууга,
Кырачаан иэстэһиигэ,
Кып-кыра, кып-кыра
Кылайбыт таҥнарыыга!

* * *

Мин дьолум буолбатах,
Мин дьоло суоҕум,
Мин баайым буолбатах,
Мин быстар дьаданым,
Мин өрөгөйүм буолбатах,
Мин курус көрүҥүм
Ымсыы дьон олоҕун сырдатар.
Дьолум кэмчи эрээри сандаарыйа,
Баайым суох эрээри дэлэмсийэ,
Курус куттаах эрээри күлэ-үөрэ
Олох устун иһэрим
Ол дьону олус да санааరһатар,
Бороҥ күннэрин өссө хараҥардар...

Natalia Kharlampieva - People's Poet of the Republic of Sakha (Yakutia).
As the author of 20 books of poetry and for many years a working
journalist, Kharlampieva is perhaps best known as the editor of the first
magazine for women in the Yakut language. Moreover, as the editor-in-
chief for a national newspaper "Sakha Sire" (The Land of Yakutia), she
arose to literary prominence across Central Asia. Indeed, as a Member
of the Writers' Union of the USSR and Russia since 1988, Winner of the
All-Russia Anton Delvig literary prize "For fidelity to the word and the
fatherland", as well as a writer awarded the Alexander Pushkin Medal,
her work continues to occupy a significant place in modern Yakut poetry.
Unsurprisingly, therefore, Kharlampieva's poems have been translated
into Russian, Kazakh, Tatar, Ukrainian and Polish

David William Parry is a published playwright, author, dramaturge, Fellow of the Royal Society of Arts, active Libertarian and Wiccan. He is the founder and chair of Theo-Humanist Arts.

By profession, Parry taught English literature, drama, language and semantics. He has given readings as a poet and practising Pagan, delivered lectures, offered sermons and performed public rituals across the United Kingdom since 1996.

HERTFORDSHIRE PRESS

Title List

Igor Savitsky:
Artist, Collector, Museum Founder
by Marinika Babanazarova (2011)

Since the early 2000s, Igor Savitsky's life and accomplishments have earned increasing international recognition. He and the museum he founded in Nukus, the capital of Karakalpakstan in the far northwest of Uzbekistan. Marinika Babanazarova's memoir is based on her 1990 graduate dissertation at the Tashkent Theatre and Art Institute. It draws upon correspondence, official records, and other documents about the Savitsky family that have become available during the last few years, as well as the recollections of a wide range of people who knew Igor Savitsky personally.

Игорь Савитский: художник, собиратель, основатель музея

С начала 2000-х годов, жизнь и достижения Игоря Савицкого получили широкое признание во всем мире. Он и его музей, основанный в Нукусе, столице Каракалпакстана, стали предметом многочисленных статей в мировых газетах и журналах, таких как TheGuardian и NewYorkTimes, телевизионных программ в Австралии, Германии и Японии. Книга издана на русском, английском и французском языках.

Igor Savitski: Peintre, collectionneur, fondateur du Musée (French), (2012)

Le mémoire de Mme Babanazarova, basé sur sa thèse de 1990 à l'Institut de Théâtre et D'art de Tachkent, s'appuie sur la correspondance, les dossiers officiels et d'autres documents d'Igor Savitsky et de sa famille, qui sont devenus disponibles dernièrement, ainsi que sur les souvenirs de nombreuses personnes ayant connu Savistky personellement, ainsi que sur sa propre expérience de travail a ses cotés, en tant que successeur designé. son nom a titre posthume.

LANGUAGE: **ENG, RUS, FR**   ISBN: **978-0955754999**   RRP: **£10.00**
AVAILABLE ON **KINDLE**

Savitsky Collection Selected Masterpieces.
Poster set of 8 posters (2014)

Limited edition of prints from the world-renowned Museum of Igor Savitsky in Nukus, Uzbekistan. The set includs nine of the most famous works from the Savitsky collection wrapped in a colourful envelope. Selected Masterpieces of the Savitsky Collection.

[Cover] BullVasily Lysenko 1. Oriental Café Aleksei Isupov 2. Rendezvous Sergei Luppov 3. By the Sea. Marie-LouiseKliment Red'ko 4. Apocalypse Aleksei Rybnikov 5. Rain Irina Shtange 6. Purple Autumn Ural Tansykbayaev 7. To the Train Viktor Ufimtsev 8. Brigade to the fields Alexander Volkov This museum, also known as the Nukus Museum or the Savitsky

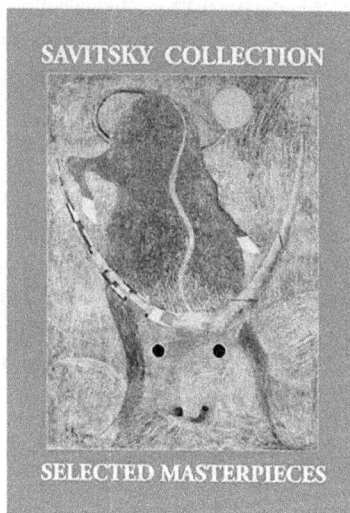

ISBN: **9780992787387**
RRP: **£25.00**

Friendly Steppes.
A Silk Road Journey
by Nick Rowan

This is the chronicle of an extraordinary adventure that led Nick Rowan to some of the world's most incredible and hidden places. Intertwined with the magic of 2,000 years of Silk Road history, he recounts his experiences coupled with a remarkable realisation of just what an impact this trade route has had on our society as we know it today. Containing colourful stories, beautiful photography and vivid characters, and wrapped in the local myths and legends told by the people Nick met and who live along the route, this is both a travelogue and an education of a part of the world that has remained hidden for hundreds of years.

HARD BACK ISBN: **978-0-9927873-4-9**
PAPERBACK ISBN: **978-0-9557549-4-4**
RRP: **£14.95**
AVAILABLE ON **KINDLE**

Birds of Uzbeksitan
by Nedosekov (2012)

FIRST
AND ONLY PHOTOALBUM
OF UZBEKISTAN BIRDS!

This book, which provides an introduction to the birdlife of Uzbekistan, is a welcome addition to the tools available to those working to conserve the natural heritage of the country. In addition to being the first photographic guide to the birds of Uzbekistan, the book is unique in only using photographs taken within the country. The compilers are to be congratulated on preparing an attractive and accessible work which hopefully will encourage more people to discover the rich birdlife of the country and want to protect it for future generations

HARD BACK
ISBN: **978-0-955754913**
RRP: **£25.00**

Pool of Stars
by Olesya Petrova,
Askar Urmanov,
English Edition (2007)

It is the first publication of a young writer Olesya Petrova, a talented and creative person. Fairy-tale characters dwell on this book's pages. Lovely illustrations make this book even more interesting to kids, thanks to a remarkable artist Askar Urmanov. We hope that our young readers will be very happy with such a gift. It's a book that everyone will appreciate. For the young, innocent ones - it's a good source of lessons they'll need in life. For the not-so-young but young at heart, it's a great book to remind us that life is so much more than work.

ISBN: **978-0955754906 ENGLISH**   AVAILABLE ON **KINDLE**

«Звёздная лужица»

Первая книга для детей, изданная британским издательством Hertfordshire Press. Это также первая публикация молодой талантливой писательницы Олеси Петровой. Сказочные персонажи живут на страницах этой книги. Прекрасные иллюстрации делают книгу еще более интересной и красочной для детей, благодаря замечательному художнику Аскару Урманову. Вместе Аскар и Олеся составляют удивительный творческий тандем, который привнес жизнь в эту маленькую книгу

ISBN: **978-0955754906   RUSSIAN**
RRP: **£4.95**

Buyuk Temurhon (Tamerlane)
by C. Marlowe,
Uzbek Edition (2010)

Hertfordshire based publisher Silk Road Media, run by Marat Akhmedjanov, and the BBC Uzbek Service have published one of Christopher Marlowe's famous plays, Tamburlaine the Great, translated into the Uzbek language. It is the first of Christopher Marlowe's plays to be translated into Uzbek, which is Tamburlaine's native language. Translated by Hamid Ismailov, the current BBC World Service Writer-in-Residence, this new publication seeks to introduce English classics to Uzbek readers worldwide.

PAPERBACK
ISBN: **9780955754982**
RRP: **£10.00**
AVAILABLE ON **KINDLE**

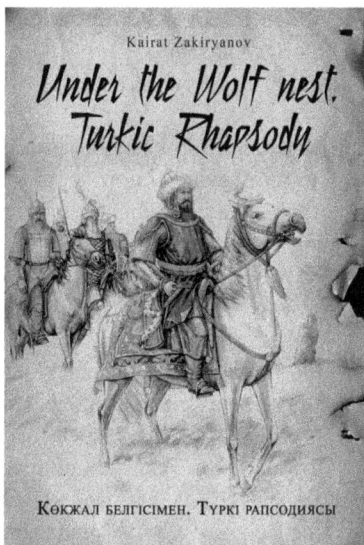

Kairat Zakiryanov

Under the Wolf nest.
Turkic Rhapsody

Көжал белгісімен. Түркі рапсодиясы

Under Wolf's Nest
by KairatZakiryanov
English –Kazakh edition

Were the origins of Islam, Christianity and the legend of King Arthur all influenced by steppe nomads from Kazakhstan? Ranging through thousands of years of history, and drawing on sources from Herodotus through to contemporary Kazakh and Russian research, the crucial role in the creation of modern civilisation played by the Turkic people is revealed in this detailed yet highly accessible work. Professor Kairat Zakiryanov, President of the Kazakh Academy of Sport and Tourism, explains how generations of steppe nomads, including Genghis Khan, have helped shape the language, culture and populations of Asia, Europe, the Middle East and America through migrations taking place over millennia.

HARD BACK
ISBN: **9780957480728**
RRP: **£17.50**
AVAILABLE ON **KINDLE**

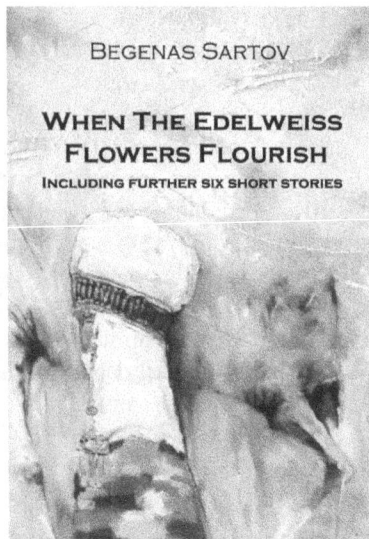

When Edelweiss flowers flourish
by Begenas Saratov
English edition (2012)

A spectacular insight into life in the Soviet Union in the late 1960's made all the more intriguing by its setting within the Sovet Republic of Kyrgyzstan. The story explores Soviet life, traditional Kyrgyz life and life on planet Earth through a Science Fiction story based around an alien nations plundering of the planet for life giving herbs. The author reveals far sighted thoughts and concerns for conservation, management of natural resources and dialogue to achieve peace yet at the same time shows extraordinary foresight with ideas for future technologies and the progress of science. The whole style of the writing gives a fascinating insight into the many facets of life in a highly civilised yet rarely known part of the world.

ISBN: **978-0955754951**   **PAPERBACK**   AVAILABLE ON **KINDLE**

Mamyry gyldogon maalda

Это фантастический рассказ, повествующий о советской жизни, жизни кыргызского народа и о жизни на планете в целом. Автор рассказывает об инопланетных народах, которые пришли на нашу планету, чтобы разграбить ее. Автор раскрывает дальновидность мысли о сохранение и рациональном использовании природных ресурсов, а также диалога для достижения мира и в то же время показывает необычайную дальновидность с идеями для будущих технологий и прогресса науки. Книга также издана на **кыргызском языке**.

ISBN: **9780955754951**
RRP: **£12.95**

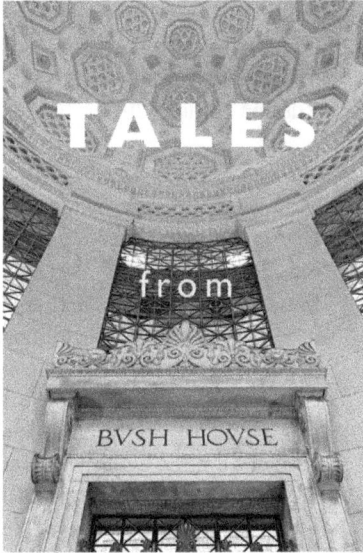

Tales from Bush House
(BBC Wolrd Service)
by Hamid Ismailov
(2012)

Tales From Bush House is a col-
lection of short narratives about
working lives, mostly real
and comic, sometimes poignant
or apocryphal, gifted to the editors
by former and current BBC World
Service employees. They are tales
from inside Bush House - the home
of the World Service since 1941 -
escaping through its marble-clad
walls at a time when its staff begin
their departure to new premises
in Portland Place. In July 2012,
the grand doors of this imposing
building will close on a vibrant chapter in the history of Britain's most
cosmopolitan organisation. So this is a timely book.

PAPERBACK
ISBN: **9780955754975**
RRP: **£12.95**
AVAILABLE ON **KINDLE**

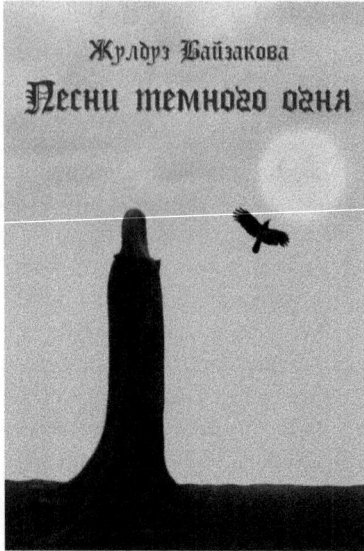

**Chants of Dark Fire
(Песни темного огня)**
by Zhulduz Baizakova
Russian edition (2012)

This contemporary work of poetry contains the deep and inspirational rhythms of the ancient Steppe. It combines the nomad, modern, postmodern influences in Kazakhstani culture in the early 21st century, and reveals the hidden depths of contrasts, darkness, and longing for light that breathes both ice and fire to inspire a rich form of poetry worthy of reading and contemplating. It is also distinguished by the uniqueness of its style and substance. Simply sublime, it has to be read and felt for real.

ISBN: **978-0957480711**
RRP: **£10.00**

Kamila
by R. Karimov
Kyrgyz – Uzbek Edition (2013)

«Камила» - это история о сироте, растущей на юге Кыргызстана. Наряду с личной трагедией Камилы и ее родителей, Рахим Каримов описывает очень реалистично и подробно местный образ жизни. Роман выиграл конкурс "Искусство книги-2005" в Бишкеке и был признан национальным бестселлером Книжной палаты Кыргызской Республики.

PAPERBACK
ISBN: **978-0957480773**
RRP: **£10.00**

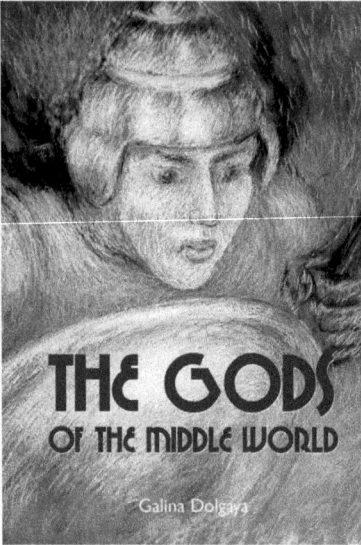

Gods of the Middle World
by Galina Dolgaya (2013)

The Gods of the Middle World tells the story of Sima, a student of archaeology for whom the old lore and ways of the Central Asian steppe peoples are as vivid as the present. When she joints a group of archaeologists in southern Kazakhstan, asking all the time whether it is really possible to 'commune with the spirits', she soon discovers the answer first hand, setting in motion events in the spirit world that have been frozen for centuries. Meanwhile three millennia earlier, on the same spot, a young woman and her companion struggle to survive and amend wrongs that have caused the neighbouring tribe to take revenge. The two narratives mirror one another, and Sima's destiny is to resolve the ancient wrongs in her own lifetime and so restore the proper balance of the forces of good and evil

PAPERBACK
ISBN: **978-0957480797**
RRP: **£14.95**
AVAILABLE ON **KINDLE**

Jazz Book, poetry
by Alma Sharipova , Russian
Edition

Сборник стихов Алмы
Шариповой JazzCafé,
в котором предлагаются
стихотворения, написанные
в разное время и посвященые
различным событиям из жизни
автора.

Стихотворения Алмы
содержательные
и эмоциональные
одновременно, отражают
философию ее отношения
к происходящему. Почти
каждое стихотворение представляет собой законченный
рассказ в миниатюре. Сюжет разворачивается последовательно
и завершается небольшим резюме в последних строках.
Стихотворения раскрываются, как готовые «формулы» жизни.
Читатель невольно задумывается над ними и может найти как
что-то знакомое, так и новое для себя.

ISBN: **978-0-957480797**
RRP: **£10.00**

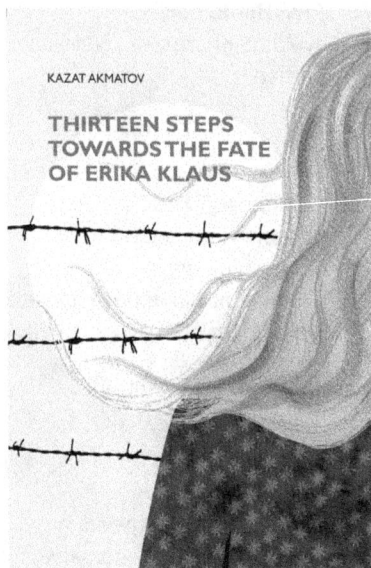

13 steps of Erika Klaus
by Kazat Akmatov (2013)

KAZAT AKMATOV

**THIRTEEN STEPS
TOWARDS THE FATE
OF ERIKA KLAUS**

The story involves the harrowing experiences of a young and very naïve Norwegian woman who has come to Kyrgyzstan to teach English to schoolchildren in a remote mountain outpost. Governed by the megalomaniac Colonel Bronza, the community barely survives under a cruel and unjust neo-fascist regime. Immersed in the local culture, Erika is initially both enchanted and apprehensive but soon becomes disillusioned as day after day, she is forbidden to teach. Alongside Erika's story, are the personal tragedies experienced by former soldier Sovietbek , Stalbek, the local policeman, the Principal of the school and a young man who has married a Kyrgyz refugee from Afghanistan . Each tries in vain, to challenge and change the corrupt political situation in which they are forced to live.

PAPERBACK
ISBN: **978-0957480766**
RRP: **£12.95**
AVAILABLE ON **KINDLE**

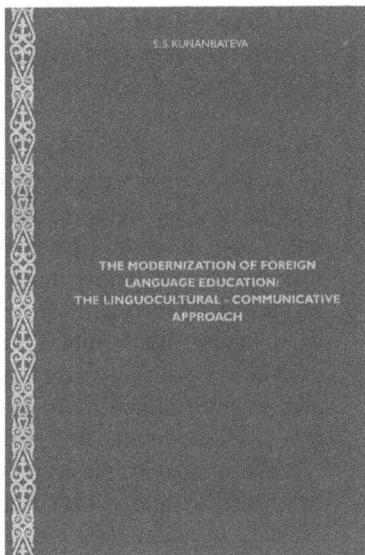

The Modernization of Foreign Language Education: The Linguocultural - Communicative Approach
by SalimaKunanbayeva (2013)

Professor S. S. Kunanbayeva - Rector of Ablai Khan Kazakh University of International Relations and World Languages This textbook is the first of its kind in Kazakhstan to be devoted to the theory and practice of foreign language education. It has been written primarily for future teachers of foreign languages and in a wider sense for all those who to be interested in the question (in the problems?) of the study and use of foreign languages. This book outlines an integrated theory of modern foreign language learning (FLL) which has been drawn up and approved under the auspices of the school of science and methodology of Kazakhstan's Ablai Khan University of International Relations and World Languages.

PAPERBACK
ISBN: **978-0957480780**
RRP: **£19.95**
AVAILABLE ON **KINDLE**

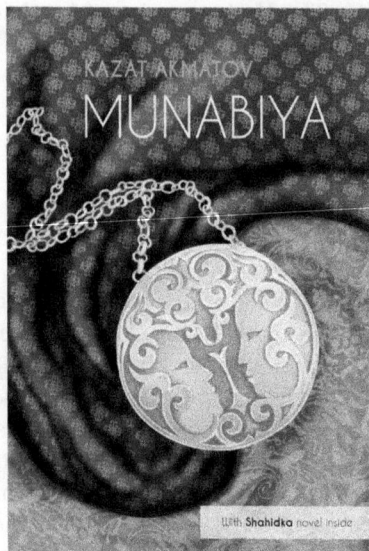

Shahidka/ Munabia
by KazatAkmatov (2013)

Munabiya and Shahidka by Kazat Akmatov National Writer of Kyrgyzstan Recently translated into English Akmatov's two love stories are set in rural Kyrgyzstan, where the natural environment, local culture, traditions and political climate all play an integral part in the dramas which unfold. Munabiya is a tale of a family's frustration, fury, sadness and eventual acceptance of a long term love affair between the widowed father and his mistress. In contrast, Shahidka is a multi-stranded story which focuses on the ties which bind a series of individuals to the tragic and ill-fated union between a local Russian girl and her Chechen lover, within a multi-cultural community where violence, corruption and propaganda are part of everyday life.

PAPERBACK
ISBN: **978-0957480759**
RRP: **£12.95**
AVAILABLE ON **KINDLE**

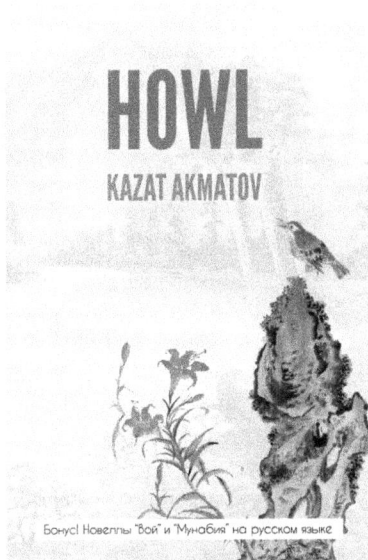

Howl *novel*
by Kazat Akmatov (2014)
English –Russian

The "Howl" by Kazat Akmatov is a beautifully crafted novel centred on life in rural Kyrgyzstan. Characteristic of the country's national writer, the simple plot is imbued with descriptions of the spectacular landscape, wildlife and local customs. The theme however, is universal and the contradictory emotions experienced by Kalen the shepherd must surely ring true to young men, and their parents, the world over. Here is a haunting and sensitively written story of a bitter -sweet rite of passage from boyhood to manhood.

PAPERBACK
ISBN: **978-0993044410**
RRP: **£12.50**
AVAILABLE ON **KINDLE**

Бонус! Новеллы "Вой" и "Мунабия" на русском языке

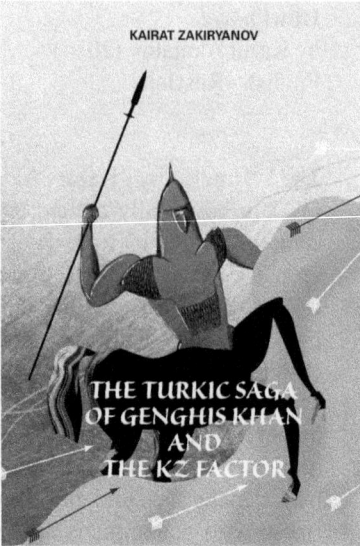

**The Turkic Saga
of Genghis Khan
and the KZ Factor**
by Dr.Kairat Zakiryanov (2014)

An in-depth study of Genghis Khan from a Kazakh perspective, The Turkic Saga of Genghis Khan presupposes that the great Mongol leader and his tribal setting had more in common with the ancestors of the Kazakhs than with the people who today identify as Mongols. This idea is growing in currency in both western and eastern scholarship and is challenging both old Western assumptions and the long-obsolete Soviet perspective. This is an academic work that draws on many Central Asian and Russian sources and often has a Eurasianist bias - while also paying attention to new accounts by Western authors such as Jack Weatherford and John Man. It bears the mark of an independent, unorthodox and passionate scholar.

HARD BACK
ISBN: **978-0992787370**
RRP: **£17.50**
AVAILABLE ON **KINDLE**

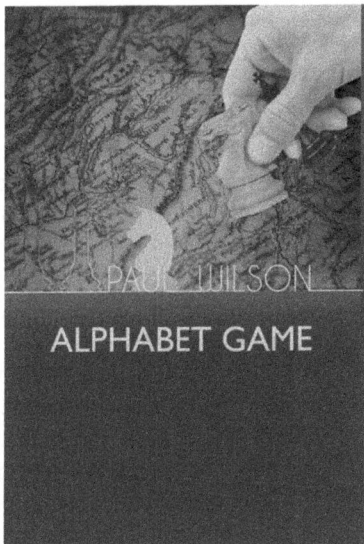

Alphabet Game
by Paul Wilson (2014)

Travelling around the world may appear as easy as ABC, but looks can be deceptive: there is no 'X' for a start. Not since Xidakistan was struck from the map. Yet post 9/11, with the War on Terror going global, could 'The Valley' be about to regain its place on the political stage? Xidakistan's fate is inextricably linked with that of Graham Ruff, founder of Ruff Guides. Setting sail where Around the World in Eighty Days and Lost Horizon weighed anchor, our not-quite-a-hero suffers all in pursuit of his golden triangle: The Game, The Guidebook, The Girl. With the future of printed Guidebooks increasingly in question, As Evelyn Waugh's Scoop did for Foreign Correspondents the world over, so this novel lifts the lid on Travel Writers for good.

PAPERBACK
ISBN: **978-0-992787325**
RRP: **£14.95**
AVAILABLE ON **KINDLE**

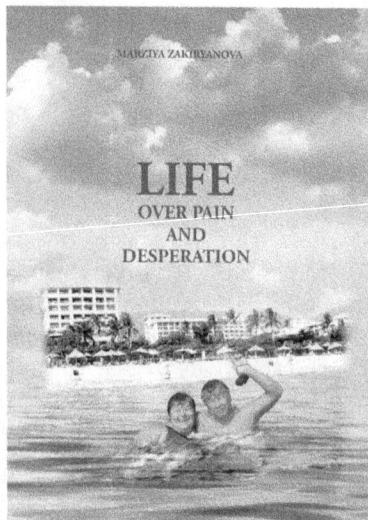

Life over pain and desperation
by Marziya Zakiryanova (2014)

This book was written by someone on the fringe of death. Her life had been split in two: before and after the first day of August 1991 when she, a mother of two small children and full of hopes and plans for the future, became disabled in a single twist of fate. Narrating her tale of self-conquest, the author speaks about how she managed to hold her family together, win the respect and recognition of people around her and above all, protect the fragile concept of 'love' from fortune's cruel turns. By the time the book was submitted to print, Marziya Zakiryanova had passed away. She died after making the last correction to her script. We bid farewell to this remarkable and powerfully creative woman.

HARD BACK
ISBN: **978-0-99278733-2**
RRP: **£14.95**
AVAILABLE ON **KINDLE**

**100 experiences
of Kazakhstan**
by Vitaly Shuptar, Nick Rowan
and Dagmar Schreiber (2014)

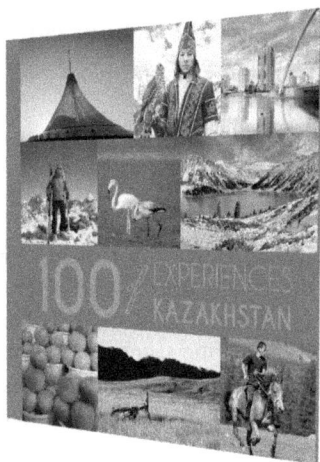

The original land of the no-
mads, landlocked Kazakhstan
and its expansive steppes pres-
ent an intriguing border be-
tween Europe and Asia. Dis-
pel the notion of oil barons
and Borat and be prepared
for a warm welcome into a land
full of contrasts. A visit to this
newly independent country
will transport you to a bygone era to discover a country full of leg-
ends and wonders. Whether searching for the descendants of Genghis
Khan - who left his mark on this land seven hundred years ago -
or looking to discover the futuristic architecture of its capital Asta-
na, visitors cannot fail but be impressed by what they experience.
For those seeking adventure, the formidable Altai and Tien Shan
mountains provide challenges for novices and experts alike

ISBN: **978-0-992787356**
RRP: **£19.95**

Dance of Devils , Jinlar Bazmi
by AbdulhamidIsmoil
and Hamid Ismailov
(Uzbek language),
E-book (2012)

'Dance of Devils' is a novel about the life of a great Uzbek writer Abdulla Qadyri (incidentally, 'Dance of Devils' is the name of one of his earliest short stories). In 1937, Qadyri was going to write a novel, which he said was to make his readers to stop reading his iconic novels "Days Bygone" and "Scorpion from the altar," so beautiful it would have been. The novel would've told about a certain maid, who became a wife of three Khans - a kind of Uzbek Helen of Troy. He told everyone: "I will sit down this winter and finish this novel - I have done my preparatory work, it remains only to write. Then people will stop reading my previous books". He began writing this novel, but on the December 31, 1937 he was arrested.

AVAILABLE ON **KINDLE**
ASIN: B009ZBPV2M

Vanished Khans and Empty Steppes by Robert Wight (2014)

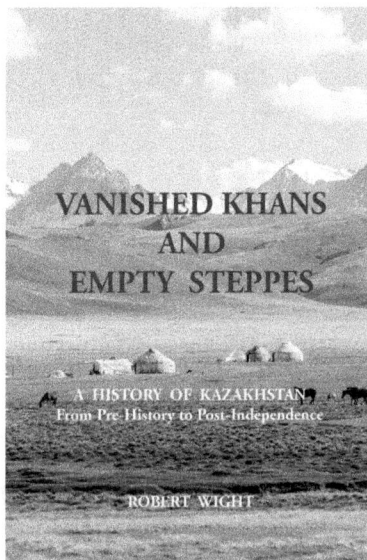

The book opens with an outline of the history of Almaty, from its nineteenth-century origins as a remote outpost of the Russian empire, up to its present status as the thriving second city of modern-day Kazakhstan. The story then goes back to the Neolithic and early Bronze Ages, and the sensational discovery of the famous Golden Man of the Scythian empire. The transition has been difficult and tumultuous for millions of people, but Vanished Khans and Empty Steppes illustrates how Kazakhstan has emerged as one of the world's most successful post-communist countries.

HARD BACK
ISBN: **978-0-9930444-0-3**
RRP: **£24.95**

PAPERBACK
ISBSN: **978-1-910886-05-2**
RRP: **£14.50**
AVAILABLE ON **KINDLE**

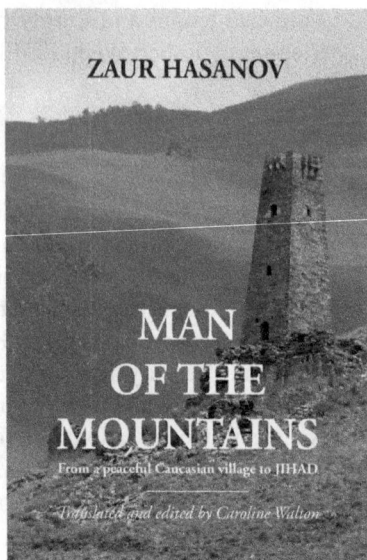

Man of the Mountains
by Abudlla Isa (2014)
(OCABF 2013 Winner)

Man of the Mountains" is a book
about a young Muslim Chechen
boy, Zaur who becomes a cen
tral figure representing the figh
of local indigenous people agains
both the Russians invading
the country and Islamic radicals
trying to take a leverage of the sit
uation, using it to push their nar
row political agenda on the eve
of collapse of the USSR. After 9/1
and the invasion of Iraq and Afghan
istan by coalition forces, the sub
ject of the Islamic jihadi movemen
has become an important subject for the Western readers. But few know
about the resistance movement from the local intellectuals and moderate
against radical Islamists taking strong hold in the area.

PAPERBACK
ISBN: **978-0-9930444-5-8**
RRP: **£14.95**
AVAILABLE ON **KINDLE**

Silk, Spice, Veils and Vodka
by Felicity Timcke (2014)

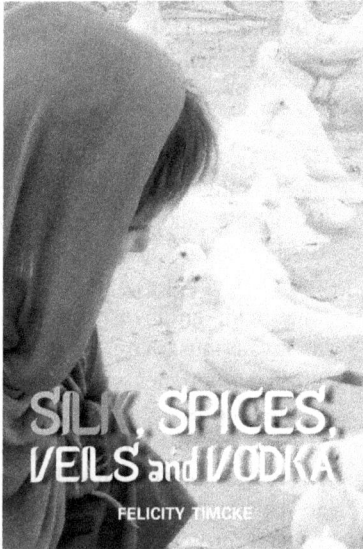

Felicity Timcke's missive publication, "Silk, Spices, Veils and Vodka" brings both a refreshing and new approach to life on the expat trail. South African by origin, Timcke has lived in some very exotic places, mostly along the more challenging countries of the Silk Road. Although the book's content, which is entirely composed of letters to the author's friends and family, is directed primarily at this group, it provides "20 years of musings" that will enthral and delight those who have either experienced a similar expatriate existence or who are nervously about to depart for one.

PAPERBACK
ISBN: **978-0992787318**
RRP: **£12.50**
AVAILABLE ON **KINDLE**

Finding the Holy Path
by Shahsanem Murray (2014)

"Murray's first book provides an enticing and novel link between her adopted home town of Edinburgh and her origins form Central Asia. Beginning with an investigation into a mysterious lamp that turns up in an antiques shop in Edinburgh, and is bought on impulse, we are quickly brought to the fertile Ferghana valley in Uzbekistan to witness the birth of Kara-Choro, and the start of an enthralling story that links past and present. Told through a vivid and passionate dialogue, this is a tale of parallel discovery and intrigue. The beautifully translated text, interspersed by regional poetry, cannot fail to impress any reader, especially those new to the region who will be affectionately drawn into its heart in this page-turning cultural thriller."

В поисках святого перевала – удивительный приключенческий роман, основанный на исторических источниках. Произведение Мюррей – это временной мостик между эпохами, который помогает нам переместиться в прошлое и уносит нас далеко в 16 век. Закрученный сюжет предоставляет нам уникальную возможность, познакомиться с историейи культурой Центральной Азии. «Первая книга Мюррей предлагает заманчивый роман, связывающий между её приемным городом Эдинбургом и Центральной Азией, откуда настоящее происхождение автора.

RUS ISBN: **978-0-9930444-8-9**
ENGL ISBN: **978-0992787394**
PAPERBACK
RRP: **£12.50**

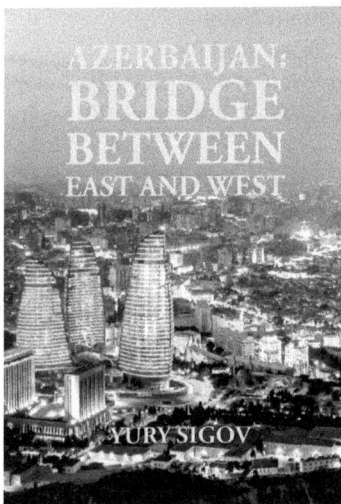

Azerbaijan:
Bridge between East and West
by Yury Sigov, 2015

Azerbaijan: Bridge between East and West, Yury Sigov narrates a comprehensive and compelling story about Azerbaijan. He balances the country's rich cultural heritage, wonderful people and vibrant environment with its modern political and economic strategies. Readers will get the chance to thoroughly explore Azerbaijan from many different perspectives and discover a plethora of innovations and idea, including the recipe for Azerbaijan's success as a nation and its strategies for the future. The book also explores the history of relationships between United Kingdom and Azerbaijan.

HARD BACK
ISBN: **978-0-9930444-9-6**
RRP: **£24.50**
AVAILABLE ON **KINDLE**

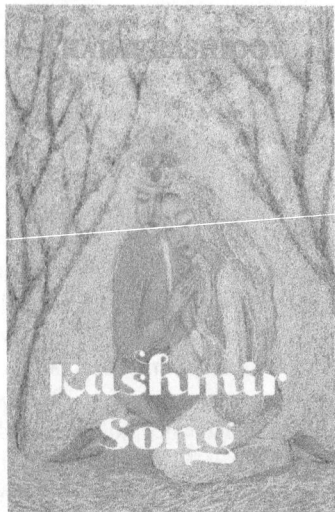

Kashmir Song
by Sharaf Rashidov
(translation by Alexey Ulko, OCABF 2014 Winner). 2015

This beautiful illustrated novella offers a sensitive reworking of an ancient and enchanting folk story which although rooted in Kashmir is, by nature of its theme, universal in its appeal.

Alternative interpretations of this tale are explored by Alexey Ulko in his introduction, with references to both politics and contemporary literature, and the author's epilogue further reiterates its philosophical dimension.

The Kashmir Song is a timeless tale, which true to the tradition of classical folklore, can be enjoyed on a number of levels by readers of all ages.

COMING SOON!!!
ISBN: 978-0-9930444-2-7
RRP: £29.50

Land of forty tribes
by Farideh Heyat, 2015

Sima Omid, a British-Iranian anthropologist in search of her Turkic roots, takes on a university teaching post in Kyrgyzstan. It is the year following 9/11, when the US is asserting its influence in the region. Disillusioned with her long-standing relationship, Sima is looking for a new man in her life. But the foreign men she meets are mostly involved in relationships with local women half their age, and the Central Asian men she finds highly male chauvinist and aggressive towards women.

PAPERBACK
ISBN: **978-0-9930444-4-1**
RRP: **£14.95**

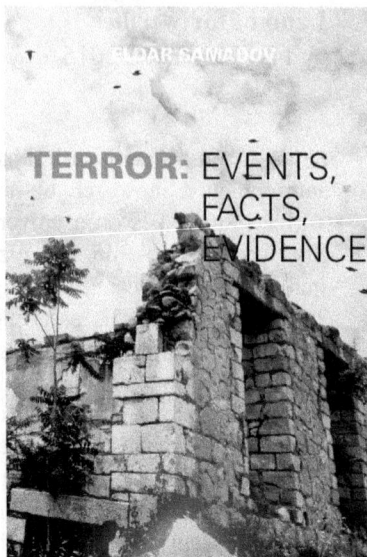

Terror: events, facts, evidence.
by Eldar Samadov, 2015

This book is based on research carried out since 1988 on territorial claims of Armenia against Azerbaijan, which led to the escalation of the conflict over Nagorno-Karabakh. This escalation included acts of terror by Armenian terrorist and other armed gangs not only in areas where intensive armed confrontations took place but also away from the fighting zones. This book, not for the first time, reflects upon the results of numerous acts of premeditated murder, robbery, armed attack and other crimes through collected material related to criminal cases which have been opened at various stages following such crimes. The book is meant for political scientists, historians, lawyers, diplomats and a broader audience.

PAPERBACK
ISBN: **978-1-910886-00-7**
RRP: **£9.99**
AVAILABLE ON **KINDLE**

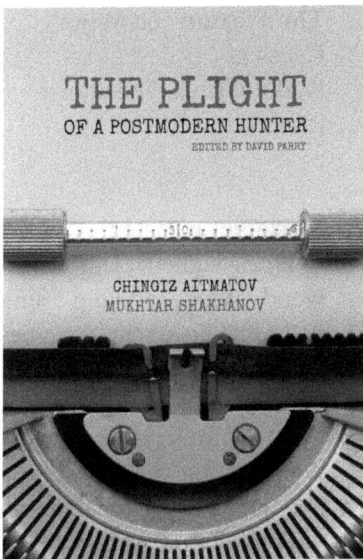

THE PLIGHT OF A POSTMODERN HUNTER

Chlngiz Aitmatov
Mukhtar Shakhanov
(2015)

"Delusion of civilization" by M. Shakhanov is an epochal poem, rich in prudence and nobility – as is his foremother steppe. It is the voice of the Earth, which raised itself in defense of the human soul. This is a new genre of spiritual ecology. As such, this book is written from the heart of a former tractor driver, who knows all the "scars and wrinkles" of the soil - its thirst for human intimacy. This book is also authored from the perspective of an outstanding intellectual whose love for national traditions has grown as universal as our common great motherland.

I dare say, this book is a spiritual instrument of patriotism for all humankind. Hence, there is something gentle, kind, and sad, about the old swan-song of Mukhtar's brave ancestors. Those who for six months fought to the death to protect Grand Otrar - famous worldwide for its philosophers and rich library, from the hordes of Genghis Khan.

LANGUAGES ENG
HARDBACK
ISBN: **978-1-910886-11-3**
RRP: **£24.95**
AVAILABLE ON **KINDLE**

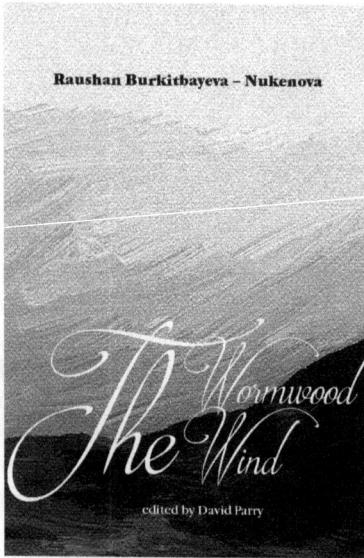

The Wormwood Wind
Raushan
Burkitbayeva- Nukenova
(2015)

A single unstated assertion runs throughout The Wormwood Wind, arguing, amid its lyrical nooks and crannies, we are only fully human when our imaginations are free. Possibly this is the primary glittering insight behind Nukenova's collaboration with hidden Restorative Powers above her pen. No one would doubt, for example, when she hints that the moment schoolchildren read about their surrounding environment they are acting in a healthy and developmental manner. Likewise, when she implies any adult who has the courage to think "outside the box" quickly gains a reputation for adaptability in their private affairs – hardly anyone would doubt her. General affirmations demonstrating this sublime and liberating contribution to Global Text will prove dangerous to unwary readers, while its intoxicating rhythms and rhymes will lead a grateful few to elative revolutions inside their own souls. Thus, I unreservedly recommend this ingenious work to Western readers.

HARD BACK
ISBN: **978-1-910886-12-0**
RRP: **£14.95**
AVAILABLE ON **KINDLE**

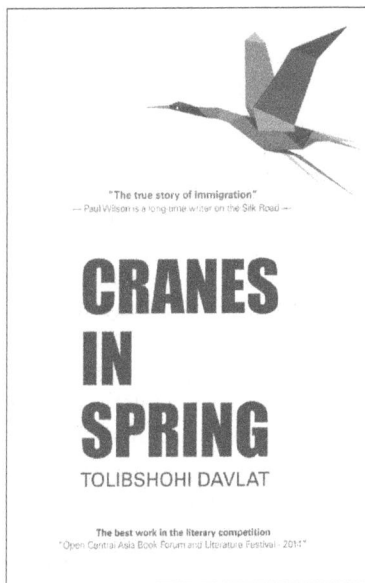

"Cranes in Spring"
by Tolibshohi Davlat
(2015)

This novel highlights a complex issue that millions of Tajiks face when becoming working migrants in Russia due to lack of opportunities at home. Fresh out of school, Saidakbar decides to go to Russia as he hopes to earn money to pay for his university tuition. His parents reluctantly let him go providing he is accompanied by his uncle, Mustakim, an experienced migrant. And so begins this tale of adventure and heartache that reflects the reality of life faced by many Central Asian migrants. Mistreatment, harassment and backstabbing join the Tajik migrants as they try to pull through in a foreign country. Davlat vividly narrates the brutality of the law enforcement officers but also draws attention to kindness and help of several ordinary people in Russia. How will Mustakim and Saidakbar's journey end? Intrigued by the story starting from the first page, one cannot put the book down until it's finished.

LANGUAGES ENG / RUS
HARDBACK
ISBN: **978-1-910886-06-9**
RRP: **£14.50**

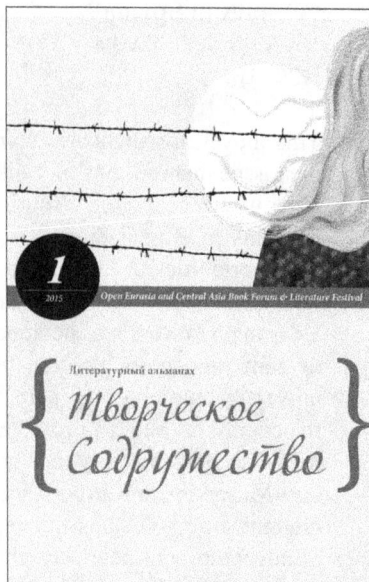

"Tvorcheskoe Sodrujestvo"
first edition
(2015)

«Творческое содружество» - это объемное издание в твердом переплете, состоящее из 500 страниц, которое включает в себя отчетный дайджест по Третьему Международному Литературному Фестивалю и Книжному Форуму «Open Eurasia and Central Asia book forum and literature festival - 2014».

В издании опубликованы фрагменты из произведений гостей фестиваля, финалистов и победителей конкурса, литературная критика, информация о мероприятиях и новинках издательства Hertfordshire Press.

LANGUAGES RUS
PAPERBACK
ISBN: **978-1910886014**
RRP: **£17.50**
HARDBACK
ISBN: **978-1910886083**
RRP: **£20**

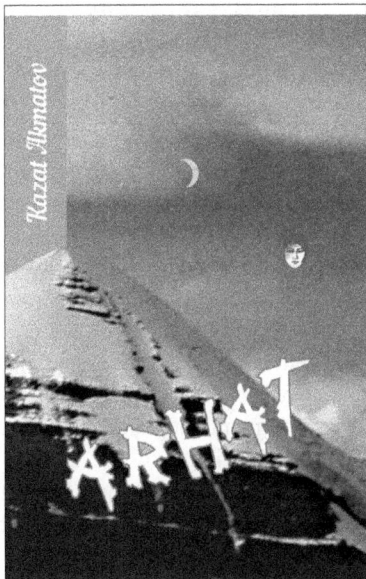

The novel "Arhat"
by Kazat Akmatov
(2015)

The novel "Arhat" by the Kyrgyz writer Kazat Akmatov was presented in Moscow at the International Festival "Bibliobraz - 2007" in the Kyrgyz, Russian and Bulgarian languages. Then, the novel was introduced to public in New Delhi at the World Buddhist Congress as well as in a city Drahsalam where the Tibetan Dalai Lama XIV lives. The novel has been translated into English and other languages. "Arhat" caused a wide resonance at home and was awarded by a number of national and international awards as well recognized the best novel and the "National bestseller of 2007". In the novel, it is a deal of the destiny of the Kyrgyz boy - the reincarnation of the great Tibetan Lama and poet who lived a thousand years ago…

LANGUAGES ENG
PAPERBACK
ISBN: **978-1910886106**
RRP: **£17.50**

Tabyldy Aktan

The Great Melody

"The Great Melody"
by Tabyldy Aktan
(2015)

"The Great Melody" is a musical drama by Tabyldy Aktan. This book is dedicated to the memory and the 150th anniversary of the great Kyrgyz bard Toktogul Satylganov. Toktogul Satulganov the Kyrgyz bard, philosopher, democrat, composer and skilled player of his country"s national instrument, the komuz, was born in 1864 in SazJuide, a village in the KetmenTobo area. In 2014 the book was translated into English by Zina Karaeva, the Director of the Institute of Foreign Languages at the International University of Kyrgyzstan.

LANGUAGES ENG
ISBN: **978-1-910886-02-1**
RRP: **£3.24**
AVAILABLE ON **KINDLE**

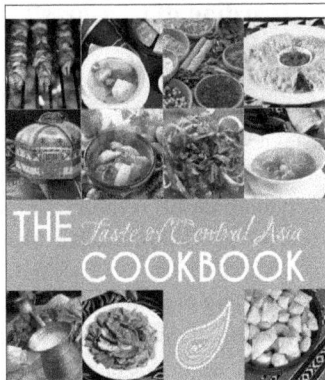

The Taste of Central asia Cook book
by Danny Gordon
(2015)

This is a culinary guide to Central Asia, divided by city and decorated with colourful images. This book is a perfect gift for those who want to discover the Central Asian region and be inspired to make new travels and gain new experiences.

LANGUAGES ENG
PAPERBACK
ISBN: **978-1-910886-09-0**
RRP: **£19.95**
COMING SOON

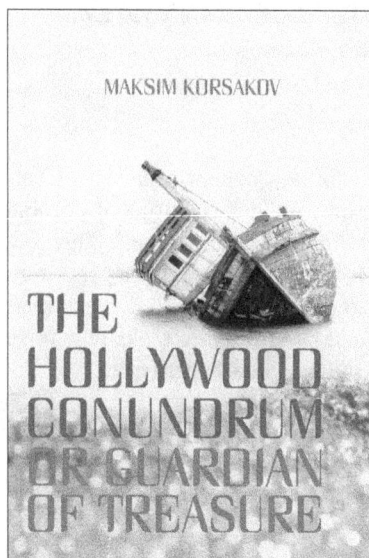

"Guardian of treasures"
by Maksim.Karsakov
(2015)

Maxim Korsakov's novella The Hollywood Conundrum or Guardian of Treasure simply refuses to acknowledge these dis-empowering parameters in anything other than the most vigorous terms. Frivolously playing, as it does, with genre expectations, and delighting in a highly crafted sensationalism. Twin techniques augmented throughout this ingenious work by Korsakov's use of texture, colour, taste, temperature, size and fleshliness. Divided into two parts, his initial tale explores the false nirvana masking marriages of convenience. A so-called "biographical" account reading like a masterclass in the muted horrors of selfimposed delusion. Immediately following, intrigued readers will discover a "script", which would easily put most James Bond screenplays to shame..

LANGUAGES ENG / RUSS
PAPERBACK
ISBN: **978-1-910886-14-4**
RRP: **£24.95**

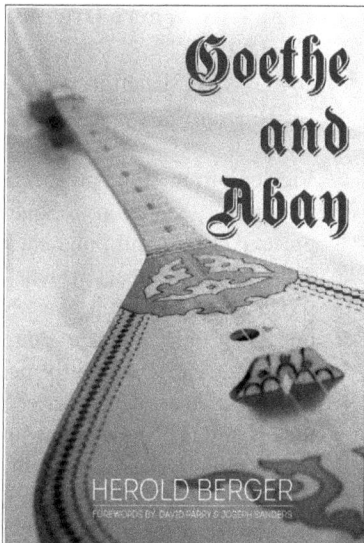

Goethe and Abai
by Herold Berger
(2015)

Present publication of Herold Berger's personal and scholarly essay on these two giants of world literature. Berger's unique stance is to follow the dictates of his imagination, inspired by a close life-long study of Goethe and Abai, and, alongside many detailed scholarly investigations, e.g. his comparative study of Goethe and Abai's innovations in poetic metre, form and consonance, or of the sources and background of Goethe's Eastern inspired masterpiece West-East Divan, Berger muses openly about the personal impact that Goethe and Abai have had on him.

LANGUAGES ENG
HARDBACK
ISBN: **978-1-910886-16-8**
RRP: **£17.50**

THE CITY
WHERE DREAMS
COME TRUE

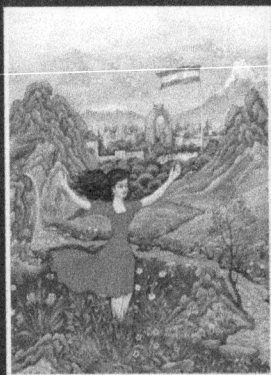

GULSIFAT SHAHIDI

"The City Where Dreams Come True"
by Gulsifat Shakhidi
(2015)

Viewed from the perspective of three generations, Shahidi presents a rare and poignant insight into the impact which Tajikistan'sterrible civil war had on its people and its culture during the early '90s. Informed partly by her own experiences as a journalist, these beautifully interwoven stories are imbued with both her affection for her native land and her hopes for its future. The narrators – Horosho, his granddaughter Nekbaht ,her husband Ali and his cousin Shernazar – each endure harrowing episodes of loss, injustice and violence but against all odds, remain driven by a will to survive, and restore peace, prosperity and new opportunities for themselves and fellow citizens.

LANGUAGES ENG / RUSS
PAPERBACK
ISBN: **978-1-910886-21-2**
RRP: **£12.50**

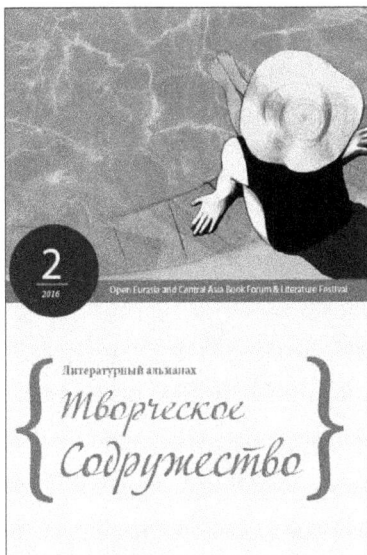

"Tvorcheskoe sodrujestvo2"
second edition
(2016)

This book is a unified voice of our generation - young and talented authors of different ethnic and cultural backgrounds. By opening this book, you discover a new artistic word, the word of writers which will pass through generations. "Creative Cooperation" reflects the literary contest «Open Eurasia and Central Asia Book Forum & Literature Festival» and seeks to enlighten, promote, and recognize the region's talents and their invaluable work.

LANGUAGES RUSS
PAPERBACK
ISBN: **978-1-910886-21-2**
RRP: **£20**